ABOVE: This beautifully illustrated 1886 map of the British Empire glorifies the wealth and exoticism of the territories then under British rule. Note: This was prior to the 'Scramble for Africa' during the last decade of the 19th century which carved up the rest of the continent between the European powers.

Welcome

England - and its successor, Great Britain - was a relative latecomer to colonialism. Its settlements in North America paled before the vast Spanish and Portuguese holdings to the south, and the French territories to the north. Gradually, as the Thirteen Colonies became more prosperous and self-sufficient, the erratic governance of the motherland became steadily more unwelcome until issues of direct taxation, land rights, and political representation erupted into revolution. Unexpectedly for Britain, the American Revolutionary War (1775–1783) ended in defeat, but this loss came at the exact same time as the British presence in India was growing in strength.

The mercantile East India Company, which managed land and people only where it was relevant to the maintenance and security of its trade 'factories' on the coast, had gotten into the business of acquiring territory almost by

accident. For close to a century, the company expanded over the Indian subcontinent with only nominal oversight from the British government until finally its clumsy mismanagement showed signs of ending the way of the Thirteen Colonies.

Instead, the aftermath of the Indian Mutiny (1857-1858) saw Great Britain take a more active role in the business of empire. What had begun as private enterprise became the jewel in an empire upon which the sun never set (because, according to one anonymous wag, an Englishman in the dark was not to be trusted.) With the exception of a European conflict roughly every half century to stir the the imperialists from complacency, over the late 18th century and well into the first decade of the 20th, the British soldier was the servant and the victim of Britain's imperial entanglements. He was called upon to conquer new lands, to put down insurrection, and to

brave malaria, dysentery, heat, and boredom whilst standing guard over remote frontiers. This living embodiment of a faraway crown and country often left much to be desired, but then so did Britain itself as it lurched from commercial cynicism to political pragmatism to naive idealism and back again, depending on who held the reins in Parliament.

As you read on you'll discover some of the key battles that altered the destiny of the empire, whether through gaining or losing territory, or changing the way that Britain viewed its place in the world, and the wider struggles which informed them.

Although its legacy is still contested and highly controversial, the British Empire shaped the British Army as much as the army shaped the empire.

James Hoare

Contents

BELOW: This colour lithograph from 1818 shows one of the many battles fought in the East India Company's conquest of the subcontinent, pitting Indian cavalry of the company's Bengal Army against the Hindu Marathas.

ABOVE: A Mahdist commander surrenders to Major Geneneral Herbert Kitchener en route to Omdurman.

Editor: James Hoare
Senior editor, specials: Roger Mortimer
Email: roger.mortimer@keypublishing.com
Design: Dan Jarman **Cover:** Lee Howson
Advertising Sales Manager: Brodie Baxter
Email: brodie.baxter@keypublishing.com
Tel: 01780 755131
Advertising Production: Rebecca Antoniades
Email: rebecca.antoniades@keypublishing.com

SUBSCRIPTION/MAIL ORDER
Key Publishing Ltd, PO Box 300,
Stamford, Lincs, PE9 1NA
Tel: 01780 480404 **Fax:** 01780 757812
Subscriptions email: subs@keypublishing.com
Mail Order email: orders@keypublishing.com
Website: www.keypublishing.com/shop

PUBLISHING
Group CEO: Adrian Cox
Publisher: Mark Elliott
Chief Publishing Officer: Jonathan Jackson
Key Publishing Ltd, PO Box 100, Stamford, Lincs, PE9 1XP
Tel: 01780 755131
Website: www.keypublishing.com

PRINTING
Precision Colour Printing Ltd, Haldane,
Halesfield 1, Telford, Shropshire. TF7 4QQ

DISTRIBUTION
Seymour Distribution Ltd, 2 Poultry Avenue,
London, EC1A 9PU
Enquiries Line: 02074 294000.

KEY PUBLISHING

Bad Company

The Battle of Plassey, June 23, 1757

Having lost ground to the belligerent Marathas - a Hindu dynasty who carved out a state in central India - and the Afghans to his northwest, the 23-year-old Nawab of Bengal, Siraj ud-Daulah, was forced to levy tougher taxes on his subjects to rebuild his shattered dominion. This included shaking down the wealthy French and British merchants, who were already eyeing each other cautiously as the Seven Years' War erupted throwing their homelands onto opposing sides.

In response, both communities began to fortify their trading posts. Siraj ud-Daulah was no friend to the British: the Honourable East India Company in Calcutta (now Kolkata) sheltered criminals from his court, their historical exemption to taxation was effectively money being taken from his purse, and now the increased militarisation of Fort William was nothing short of provocation. Siraj ud-Daulah demanded the French and British both desist in their sabre-rattling. The French obeyed, but the British did not.

On June 16, 1746, the armies of the nawab marched into Calcutta and on June 20 took Fort William after only token resistance from the garrison. The Indian levies had fled leaving fewer than 170 soldiers under the command of former army surgeon John Zephaniah Holwell to hold off the Bengalis. Against an army of 50,000 men with 500 war elephants, Holwell had no choice but to capitulate with what he claimed was a guarantee of clemency from Siraj ud-Daulah himself. ➤➤

BELOW: Major Robert Clive receives the tribute of Mir Jafar, soon to be the newly-minted Nawab of Bengal, in the wake of the Battle of Plassey.

ABOVE: An unsigned 1810 watercolour of the 13th Madras Native Infantry - raised in 1776 - wearing the uniform familiar to the Lal Pultan.

From 1600, the Honourable East India Company held the English Crown's exclusive charter to trade in Asia and along with similar merchant companies dispatched by Britain's European rivals, they established a series of warehouses, factories (trading posts) and forts along the coast. The British set themselves up at Madras in 1639, Bombay (now Mumbai) in 1668, and finally, Calcutta (now Kolkata) in 1696. These three bases were later known as presidencies, each governed independently from the other by a president and answering to the company headquarters in London.

The coming of Europe's rapine merchant-adventurers coincided with the decline of the Mughal Empire which had dominated the Indian subcontinent since the 16th century. From 1717, the EIC was granted tariff-free trade allowing its agents to purchase enormous quantities of local goods - pepper, spices, sugar, indigo dye, saltpetre, silk, and cotton - and accrue vast profits at India's expense. By 1740, EIC contributions made up 10 per cent of the entire public revenues of the British state.

As the Mughal state grew weaker, regional rulers called nawabs (from where we get 'nabob') became increasingly autonomous and ambitious. Favour became a buyer's market. As Britain and France snapped at each other on the world stage, the tensions unleashed in Europe by the War of the Austrian Succession (1740-1748) and then the Seven Years' War (1756-1763) was echoed

by the three Carnatic Wars between the rival British and French merchant companies. Fought over India's eastern coast, the first two Carnatic Wars confined the French to a single holding at Pondichéry (now Puducherry) and ensured a British client was securely ensconced as Nawab of the Carnatic thanks to the daring Captain Robert Clive, later mythologised as 'Clive of India'.

Soldiers were recruited in Britain for the Bombay, Bengal and Madras (European) Regiments, the private armies of the East India Company. During the First Carnatic War (1746-1748), France had made effective use of locally-raised troops alongside its European armies. The East India Company took note and the first regular battalion of Indian troops - called sepoys (from the Persian word for an infantryman) - was raised in January 1757 in time to prove their worth at the Battle of Plassey during the Third Carnatic War (1756-1763). The sepoys wore red coats over a white shirt with a blue cummerbund around their waist. On their lower halves, they wore white shorts, whilst officers (and sepoys in colder weather) wore pantaloons. Aside from their bare legs, their most striking and exotic feature was their pointed 'sundial' hats, replaced with a turban in the early 1800s. The Lal Pultan (Red Battalion) - as the sepoys called themselves - were later designated 1st Bengal Native Infantry but retained the battle honour 'Plassey' as a tribute to their unique vintage amongst the regiments of British India.

ABOVE: An 18th century portrait of Alivardi Khan, Siraj ud-Daulah's grandfather and predecessor as the Nawab of Bengal from 1740 to 1756.

Some 64 British and Anglo-Indian prisoners - Holwell amongst them - were rounded up and crammed into the fort's prison, a stone cell only 14 by 18 feet. Already known as the Black Hole of Calcutta to the company garrison, it was soon to enter infamy. Overnight, in suffocatingly hot conditions with little water, the prisoners trampled over each other in their desperation to take gulps of stagnant night air from the two small windows. When the cell was unlocked the next morning, only 21 remained alive. Holwell, whose published account horrified the British public and underwrote the East India Company's desire for vengeance, inflated the numbers to a physically impossible 146 inmates. Siraj ud-Daulah's days on the throne were now limited.

Throwing Down the Gauntlet

Lieutenant Colonel Robert Clive was the 32-year-old wunderkind of the East India Company. He had recently returned to India from Britain as MP for one of the country's notorious 'rotten boroughs' of a mere 55 eligible voters and he moved quickly once the slow exchange of diplomatic hot air achieved nothing. British battleships advanced up the Hooghly River from Madras, shelling first the fort at Baj-Baj and then Calcutta, taking both with ease. Clive's antics invited Siraj ud-Daulah to return to the field and he brought up an estimated 40,000 men to eject the British from Calcutta. After holding the Bengalis off, under the cover of both night and fog, Clive landed a mixture of soldiers, sailors, and Indian sepoys further downriver and attacked the Bengali camp in the early hours of February 5, 1757.

Known as the 'Calcutta Gauntlet,' the British force fought through the Bengali lines to re-enter the besieged city, leaving a trail of destruction and panic in their wake. Clive reported 57 killed and 137 wounded, whilst the Bengali casualties were estimated to be 600. The damage to morale was arguably greater and Siraj ud-Daulah sulkily signed the Treaty of Alinagar. This handed

ABOVE: The nawab's soldiers torment their prisoners in this Victorian depiction of the Black Hole of Calcutta.

Calcutta back to British control, agreed to pay the East India Company damages, and restore the economic privileges he had attempted to curtail.

With the Seven Years' War now in full swing and the French having resumed their customary role as Britain's arch-foes as well as the EIC's commercial competitors, Clive - with what he claimed was the nawab's permission - besieged and captured the French trading post at Chandannagar.

"Overnight, in suffocatingly hot conditions with little water, the prisoners trampled over each other in their desperation to take gulps of stagnant air..."

BELOW: The East India Company's Fort William headquarters in Calcutta, an etching from 1754.

Rather than allowing the British free rein, Siraj ud-Daulah attempted to lend his support to the defenders.

Ignoring his orders to return to Madras, Clive was now firmly convinced that the company would benefit from a regime change and he courted a rival. Mir Jafar, Siraj ud-Daulah's uncle and the commander of his armies, had gathered around himself a conspiracy of influential Bengalis who sought to oust the nawab from his throne.

Enormous sums of money were promised to all involved and finally, Mir Jafar put pen to paper and signed a covert agreement with Clive.

Mir Jafar's home was being watched and Siraj ud-Daulah strongly suspected Clive was scheming against him, although he clearly underestimated the scope of his uncle's involvement. Determined to put the EIC in their place once and for all, he marched his forces to the village of Palashi - called Plassey by the British - which blocked the route to his capital, Murshidabad. There they camped behind an earthen redoubt. The Bengali army consisted of 30,000 infantry, 20,000 cavalry, and 50 cannon of various sizes - some so heavy that they were mounted on wooden platforms pulled by oxen and flanked by war elephants. At Siraj ud-Daulah's elbow were 50 highly trained French artillerymen with six field guns, led by an officer called St. Frais.

On June 13 - despite the odds being stacked firmly against them and prevarication from the slippery Mir Jafar – the East India Company forces sailed up

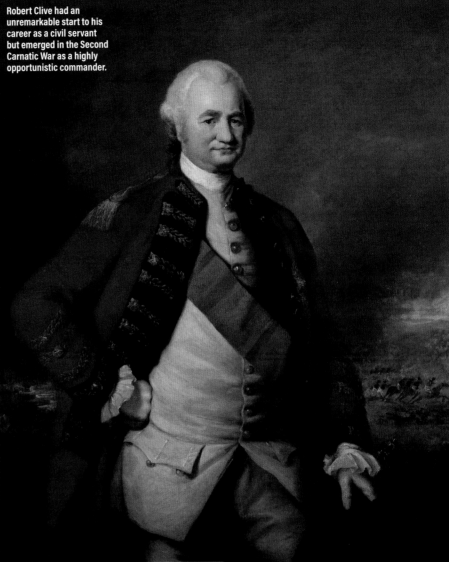

Robert Clive had an unremarkable start to his career as a civil servant but emerged in the Second Carnatic War as a highly opportunistic commander.

the Hooghly River towards Palashi. Their force comprised approximately 2,000 Indian sepoys, 1,000 company troops and British regulars of Major Eyre Coote's 39th Regiment of Foot, and 200 artillerymen with eight 6-pdr guns and two howitzers. A third of the Bengali army was under the direct command of Mir Jafar, but his disloyalty was looking as dangerously elastic as his loyalty.

Murder Among the Mangos

In the small hours of June 23, 1757, the British landed in an orchard of mango trees called Laksha Bagh, their branches drooping like willows with the weight of their thick green leaves and their succulent fruits. The grove was protected on two sides by the bend of the Hooghly and on the remaining two by an earthen wall and ditch. Even by darkness, it was clear that they risked being overwhelmed by a numerically superior force and Clive's confidence was dented. Only after he disappeared into the mangos in tense contemplation did his eagerness to fight seem restored. ➤➤

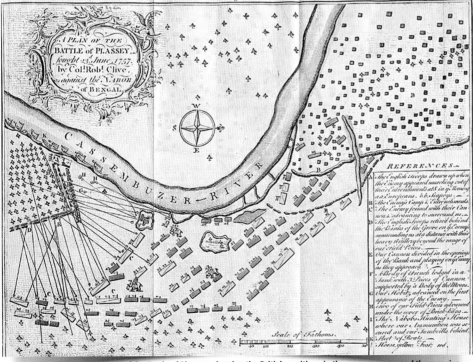

ABOVE: A contemporary map of the Battle of Plassey, showing the British positions in the mango grove, and the massive Bengali force which surrounded them.

ABOVE: A Victorian illustration showing the heavy guns of the Bengali army mounted on wooden platforms, pulled by oxen.

by the trees Siraj ud-Daulah assumed they too had been rendered inoperable by the sudden downpour. Drawing his sword, Mir Madan led his cavalry forward in a line making them ready to charge when he was blasted from his steed by grapeshot, dying shortly afterwards. The pride of Bengal bloodied by the British cannon, Siraj ud-Daulah dropped to his knees and begged Mir Jafar to intercede - no doubt enjoying the spectacle, he agreed. As Siraj ud-Daulah left Mir Jafar's tent, another of the conspirators took the ruler to one side and suggested he withdraw his men behind their entrenchments and leave the battle to his generals. The nawab galloped from the battlefield, with his men peeling off behind him. For those who looked to their leader for direction, the sight of him riding off was enough to convince them the battle was over.

The Killing Blow

As the British emerged from behind their walls they discovered that only the French artillerymen and the loyal Bengalis on the right

At dawn, the Bengali right - the French on a redoubt dug in front of the entrenchment, and behind them Siraj ud-Daulah's most trusted commanders - began to advance on the orchard through the thick humid fog. The left and centre too emerged from the camp and curved around the British position, turning on a small hill as if it were a hinge. Clive ordered his own men forward to meet the Bengali right, leaving only a token force - nowhere near enough men to see off a determined assault - to guard their flanks.

At 8am, the Franco-Bengali guns opened up and the British pieces struggled to match them, being significantly lighter and far fewer in number. Realising that he risked his entire force being whittled down by round shot, Clive pulled his men back to the safety of the orchard where the earthen walls - sodden with rain - took the impact of the cannonballs with barely

ABOVE: The lighter British guns return fire from the protection of the mango trees.

ABOVE: Major Eyre Coote of the 39th Regiment of Foot, the first regular British Army regiment to serve in India.

a tremble. From the cover, the British guns began to make a better account of themselves against the advancing enemy.

Whilst the loyal generals on the Bengali right - Mir Madan, his artillery commander, and Dirwan Mohanlal, his Hindu chief minister (whose elevation despite his faith had put Mir Jafar's nose out of joint) - pushed on, the centre and the left under the control of Mir Jafar held fast. It is impossible to decipher the traitor's intentions at this stage, but perhaps he was hedging his bets until the fate of the battle looked to have been decided one way or another.

At noon, a thunderstorm suddenly crackled into life above the battlefield and for half-an-hour, the guns fell silent as the rain soaked the Bengali fuses and powder. The British guns, meanwhile, had been covered with tarpaulin to protect them from the elements but concealed

flank still fought on in a desperate rearguard action, the latter pulling back behind their camp entrenchments, whilst the French clung fiercely to their redoubt.

Mir Jafar meanwhile began to bring the left flank down towards the mango grove, treating Clive to the horrifying spectacle of a solid third of the Bengali army advancing towards him just as the rest of them seemed to be in retreat. Not realising those were Mir Jafar's men (the traitor had sent a messenger, but he hadn't made it across the killing field), a detachment was detailed to drive them off and protect the baggage train which he assumed were the object of their attention. As the British cannon boomed, Mir Jafar wisely elected to pull his men back.

For Clive, this final push towards the entrenched positions - which crackled with fire

A 19th century watercolour by E. S. Hardy showing British infantry charging from the mango grove to confront the Bengalis.

> ## "No longer just a heavy-handed merchant enterprise, the EIC was now in the business of deposing rulers and governing territory."

from the Bengali matchlocks - was the deadliest and most dangerous phase. Once he realised that the division idling to his right was that of the nawab's treacherous uncle, he concentrated his efforts on the French redoubt and the hill which split Mir Jafar's forces from the rest of the Bengali line. Maj Coote's grenadier companies - the most physically imposing men of the 39th Foot - took the hill, its defenders giving it up without firing a single round. Eventually even the dogged St. Frais was forced to withdraw his tiring French artillerymen from their redoubt, dragging their smoking guns behind them.

By 5pm, Clive had taken the Bengali camp and entrenchments at a total cost of 22 killed and 50 wounded, the casualties inflicted on his enemy being considerably higher. The next evening, Clive met with Mir Jafar and proclaimed him Nawab of Bengal. Now on the run and meeting only defeatism in his capital, Siraj ud-Daulah made it as far as Rajmahal where he was murdered by Mir Jafar's son - his first cousin - and his cadaver was paraded through the street.

For the Honourable East India Company, the Battle of Plassey marked the end of French influence in Bengal and the beginning of British imperial power in India. No longer just a heavy-handed merchant enterprise, the EIC was now in the business of deposing rulers and governing territory. Mir Jafar - having learned nothing from the fate of his nephew - eventually enlisted Dutch support in attempting to unpick the insidious British influence, but was, in turn, defeated at the Battle of Chinsurah (November 24/25, 1759) and replaced by a more pliant puppet king - the first of many.

ABOVE: The Leadenhall Street, London headquarters of the Honourable East India Company in 1800

Paths of Glory

Battle of the Plains of Abraham, September 13, 1759

Since the outbreak of war in Europe, Great Britain had bolstered its forces in North America at the same time as France was forced to prioritise battlefields much closer to home. "One should not try and save the stables when the house was on fire," said the Minister of Marine, Nicolas René Berryer, Comte de La Ferrière. The Royal Navy, as well as driving off their French counterparts in the Atlantic, had successfully blockaded Canada, cutting off the French

garrison in their capital of Quebec from reinforcements and resupply.

At 32 years of age, Major General James Wolfe was already set to eclipse his father, Lieutenant General Edward Wolfe. An aggressive and innovative commander, Wolfe came to the attention of the prime minister, William Pitt, for his role in the amphibious 'Raid on Rochefort' and Pitt earmarked him for the invasion of Canada. The Siege of Louisbourg (June 8 – July 28, 1758) - in which Brigadier General Wolfe

led a brigade in securing the harbour entrance - successfully laid the riverine approach to Quebec bare. With naval superiority at their back, the British spent the rest of the year policing the Atlantic coast of Canada, occupying what is now New Brunswick, Prince Edward Island and Newfoundland, and ejecting a huge number of French-speaking settlers, called Acadians. (They would go onto settle around French Louisiana and become known as 'Cajuns'). ➤➤

BELOW: 'The Death of General Wolfe' by Benjamin West, 1770. Note the almost religious composition that presents Wolfe as a Christ-like figure.

ABOVE: A romanticised 19th-century depiction of Washington taking charge at the Battle of the Monongahela.

Britain's Thirteen Colonies in North America had grown rapidly since their settlement across the 16th and 17th centuries until by 1740 their total population numbered one million souls scattered between the Appalachian Mountains and the eastern seaboard. This was a primarily agrarian population and the search for ever more favourable farmland pushed them further west over the dividing ridge of the Appalachians which separated the territory claimed by Great Britain from the vast inland swathe of 'New France', the French colony of Canada and the North American interior.

Wherever the fringes of the British and French empires touched, conflict sharpened its flint but the outbreak of the French and Indian War (1754 – 1763) had just as much to do with competition for resources as it did imperial rivalry. British settlers increasingly edged west into the Ohio River Valley, both a trade artery which potentially plugged the northern colonies into the mighty Mississippi (which linked New France to French Louisiana in the south) and a source of fertile farmland. Both communities had indigenous allies, each side exploiting their European benefactor's rivalries to redress their own grievances.

In 1753 the French began to erect a chain of forts in order to enforce the French monarch's claim to the Ohio Valley. In 1754, they toppled the fortified British trading post on the vital fork where the Rivers Allegheny and Monongahela merged to form the Ohio and erected the more substantial Fort Duquesne. This was a shot across the bows of the Ohio Company of Virginia, which had been granted permission by King George II to claim land that wasn't his

A portrait of George Washington from 1772, showing him in the uniform of the Virginia Regiment.

to give away, and the governor of Virginia dispatched the militia, under the 22-year-old Colonel George Washington (whose brothers were investors in the Ohio Company, along with the governor) to renew their claim.

Washington and the Virginia Regiment stumbled across a small French Canadian party in their camp, killing ten and taking 21 captive - many of whom were later ritually murdered by Britain's Native American allies. This party, it transpired, was a diplomatic mission with the intent to settle the business of British and French sparring along the Ohio, and amongst the dead was the French ambassador.

The Battle of Jumonville Glen (May 28, 1754) - the first engagement of the French and Indian War - was followed by the humiliating defeat of Washington at his hastily-assembled Fort Necessity. Only when British reinforcements arrived under the unbending Major General Edward Braddock - who took Washington as his aide - did he get a chance to redeem himself by rescuing at least some of the Virginia Regiment from an ambush that Braddock had wandered blithely into. Inconclusive sparring along the frontiers by rival militias continued until the conflict was swallowed up by the Seven Years' War (1756-1763) which forced France (and its allies, Spain and Austria) to focus on the European theatre and the threat posed by the Prussians under King Frederick the Great. With the Royal Navy to support its operations globally, Great Britain went on the offensive in India (see page 6) and North America.

F.Turin pinx!.   R.Purcel.fecit.

Major General Wolfe.

Who, at the Expence of his Life, purchas'd immortal Honour for his Country, and planted. with his own Hand, the British Laurel, in the inhospitable Wilds of NORTH AMERICA. By the Reduction of Quebec, Sept.ʳ 13.ᵗʰ 1759.

printed for Eliz:ᵗʰ Bakewell & Hen: Parker, opposite Birchin Lane Cornhill.

Following the actions of the previous year, Lieutenant General Louis-Joseph de Montcalm, Marquis de Saint-Veran - the aristocratic commander of the French forces in North America - had been preparing for war to arrive on his doorstep. Militiamen from across New France had been mobilised for the defence of their capital and Montcalm had ordered a ten-mile wide line of redoubts and trenches dug to the east of the city, converging on Beauport where he believed a British landing most likely. The walls of Quebec had been reinforced with 109 cannon, and around 15,000 men - mostly militia - were camped in wait.

The mathematics of a siege strongly favour the attacker only when his forces vastly outnumber those behind the walls, and this is most definitely not the case. Less hopeful yet, Wolfe's appointment with destiny clashed with his looming demise. Bedridden with seasickness, rheumatism, and consumption - now known as tuberculosis, it had taken the life of his brother in 1744 - his mood had grown noticeably fatalistic even before the crossing. He took comfort from his favourite poem, *Elegy Written in a Country Churchyard* by Thomas Gray (1751) and underlined one particular verse:

> "The boast of heraldry, the pomp of pow'r,
> And all that beauty, all that wealth e'er gave,
> Awaits alike th' inevitable hour.
> The paths of glory lead but to the grave."

LEFT: A colour mezzotint of Major General James Wolfe "who, at the expense of his life, purchased immortal honour." Note the map of Quebec by his right elbow.

BELOW: A map showing the British operations and the French positions around Quebec and the St Lawrence River.

Appointed major general in 1759, Wolfe was placed at the head of a force of some 9,000 fighting men and returned to Louisbourg for the Quebec Expedition. Almost a quarter of the entire Royal Navy - 22 ships-of-the-line, 27 frigates, and 200 transports - was under the command of Admiral Sir Charles Saunders and included amongst his officers Lieutenant James Cook. The future Pacific explorer was then a 31-year-old master (an officer responsible for navigation) aboard HMS *Pembroke* and his work in surveying the mouth of the St Lawrence River was vital to the success of the coming offensive.

Much Sound and Fury

Quebec was a formidable natural fastness. The citadel's thick walls were additionally protected by sheer cliffs to the south which dropped away into the St Lawrence, and by the St Charles River, a tributary which peeled off to the northwest, surrounding Quebec on three sides by water.

ABOVE: A 1780 engraving shows the British landing craft crossing the St Lawrence and the distant ascent of the cliffs towards the Plains of Abraham.

To the delight of Montcalm, Wolfe ordered an amphibious landing on the heavily entrenched beaches around Beauport. On July 31, 4,000 redcoats tried and failed, paddling limply back to their starting points with heavy casualties. Humiliated and enraged, Wolfe lashed out and dispatched raiding parties over a 100-mile range along the southern banks of the St Lawrence, burning farms, slaughtering livestock, and levelling entire communities. With supplies already perilously low in Quebec, Wolfe's malice hastened starvation but time was working against the British too: disease was racing through the camp and by autumn the fleet would have to return to Britain or risk being imprisoned by the harsh Canadian winter. Reluctantly, Wolfe allowed his commanders to talk him into attempting a landing 30 miles further upriver, but rainfall forced them to delay. As the landing parties huddled together and waited for the sky to clear, Wolfe walked up and down the shore studying Quebec through his telescope.

He decided on an operation much closer to the city walls, one which must have struck his horrified subordinates as a looming disaster on the scale of the landing at Beauport. Under the cover of night on September 12, redcoats crossed the St Lawrence on their shallow-bottomed landing craft to a cove Wolfe had spotted through his eyeglass. Barely a mile from the city walls, they ascended a narrow goat path up 200-feet of sheer cliff face.

As dawn broke on September 13, 1759, Montcalm was stunned to discover that 4,441 British soldiers were forming up right under his nose in an overgrown meadow known as the Plains of Abraham which dominated a plateau to the immediate southwest. ➤➤

On June 26, the British fleet anchored in the St Lawrence and troops were disgorged onto the Île d'Orléans, a pastoral island in the estuary. With months spent preparing for their arrival, Montcalm struck first and as night fell a chain of 80 fire-ships packed with explosives were released into the current and carried towards the suddenly vulnerable pride of the Royal Navy. The fearsome spectacle of almost a mile-wide arc of flame yielded less than impressive results as they detonated too early, leaving nothing but a few smouldering husks to worry the Tars, their knuckles whitening in the grip of buckets of sand and water.

By July 12, the British guns were finally in position on the southern bank opposite Quebec, and Wolfe ordered them open up on the city. An estimated 50 houses in the Lower Town were destroyed by the first night's bombardment alone, but as with the French fire ships, the results were far less impressive than the pyrotechnics. The majority of the city's civilians had already packed up their belongings and escaped the range of the British guns for safer refuge inland. Nonetheless, the ailing Wolfe was resolved to pummel Quebec into submission and over nine weeks some 20,000 cannonballs were spent on what amounted to little more than industrial-scale vandalism.

Out of the Frying Pan

Wolfe's indecisiveness, ill-health and failing strategy of attrition was being looked at increasingly askance by his senior staff, who pressed their commander to land troops further upriver and advance inland on Quebec from the west. His success at Louisbourg the previous year had been an aggressive frontal assault, but it had succeeded in spite of the odds and not, as perhaps Wolfe had begun to suspect, because of some gift he had for war.

ABOVE: Whilst Wolfe and his staff watch from the cliff edge, British grenadiers ascend the goat path by the light of dawn. Oil by Frank Otis Small, 1903.

Montcalm Before the Storm

Wolfe's position was a precarious one indeed. A mile to his east was Quebec itself, but beyond that Montcalm's formidable force around Beauport was only an hour's march away. To the British rear, thousands of militiamen were strung out along the northern banks of the St Lawrence to oppose any British crossing and they could be mobilised in hours to crush the attackers. Britain's victory or defeat depended entirely on Montcalm's reaction.

The man who had, until now, predicted each of Wolfe's moves like a chess master was stunned into indecision by the suddenness and apparent foolhardiness of the manoeuvre. Uncertain as to whether this was a distraction, with a secondary landing planned elsewhere, he decided to bring up 5,000 men from Beauport, leaving the rest to hold the defences there and ordered the militia further west to hold their ground until the situation became clearer. No doubt a relief to the battalion of light infantry deployed to the British rear to hold them up.

Opposed only by a handful of militia and Native American sharpshooters who took pot-shots from the treeline, Wolfe ordered his men into two thin lines, rather than the regulation three - the preferred depth for British infantry in the field as it gave them enough weight of numbers to withstand a charge. He also ordered each man to load two musket balls rather than one, the loss of accuracy in an already inaccurate weapon largely meaningless in a wall of fire that would stretch out for almost a mile.

As the French formed up, British cannon pockmarked their lines so that by the time they advanced in one great column - the preferred French formation for breaking a line of infantry - they were already in disorder. The British, meanwhile, were sheltered by a ridge so that the French artillery was unable to wreak similar havoc on Wolfe's precision deployment. The situation was worsened by the large number of French Canadian militia, who had little in the way of drill and no experience of fighting in concert like regular infantry. As the French column marched, the broken ground of the meadow unravelled their ranks further, and mistakenly part of the lines halted to fire a

ABOVE: A heroic colour mezzotint of Wolfe directing the British assault.

"He also ordered each man to load two musket balls rather than one, the loss of accuracy in an already inaccurate weapon largely meaningless..."

BELOW: A rather busy panorama of the battle, showing Quebec in the background and the British fleet anchored in the St Lawrence River. Hand-coloured engraving from 1795.

MORT DU MARQUIS DE MONTCALM GOZON

Dediée au *Roi*

ABOVE: A curious counterpoint to the various depictions of Wolfe's death is this French copper engraving from 1761 showing the death of Lieutenant General Louis-Joseph de Montcalm, Marquis de Saint-Veran. Presumably produced by someone with a woolly understanding of Canada given the palm tree.

meaningless volley from extreme range, before resuming their progress. Now irreparably staggered, at 40 yards the French fired a volley into the British lines opposite and as they reloaded, the British returned. The devastating British volley, a mile-wide storm of lead, tore through the French lines like thunder. Barely was there a moment's silence when the pipes of the 78th (Highland) Regiment of Foot (or the Fraser Highlanders, a short-lived battalion raised for service in North America) wailed their discordant squall, on the right of the British line claymores were drawn and muskets tossed aside, and through the smoke came the flash of blades. At their back, the drums beat up the advance and the wall of red moved as one, bayonets levelled and officers bellowing encouragement.

The French Canadians broke first, fleeing before the Highlanders, and soon the entire French line was in disarray. After barely 15 minutes of fighting, the Battle of the Plains of Abraham was over. Whilst his men charged onwards, a musket ball struck Wolfe in the chest, sparing him a slow death from consumption,

and shortly afterwards Montcalm was hit below the ribs. Wolfe lived long enough to know he had delivered a victory and Montcalm died the following day, with time enough to contemplate his defeat. Fittingly given the fate of their commanders, the casualties were relatively matched with approximately 650 on either side.

That night, the French garrison at Quebec and Beauport withdrew, leaving the broken heart of New France to the enemy.

The Wonderful Year

Wolfe's remains were returned to Britain in reverence and were greeted with a level of patriotic grieving that would only be eclipsed by Admiral Horatio Nelson in 1805. His premature death at the tender age of 32 perhaps spared him a more critical appraisal of his decisions and had he lived long enough to repeat his more costly blunders then his reputation would have been very different. However, with his health so dire, perhaps all of James Wolfe's 'paths to glory' did indeed 'lead but to the grave'.

One of the many victories that led to 1759 being

christened the 'Annus Mirabilis' - the 'wonderful year' immortalised in the Royal Navy march, *Hearts of Oak* - the victory at the Battle of the Plains of Abraham delivered Quebec to the British, but keeping it was a more torturous endeavour.

Both the British garrison and the townsfolk were left to face the winter in the ruins left by Wolfe's bombardment, united by their misery and hunger. After regrouping in Montreal, the French besieged the survivors in turn in 1760, but whilst the Royal Navy continued to blockade the North Atlantic and the Kingdom of France had no choice but to concentrate the fight in Europe, New France was doomed. The terms of the Treaty of Paris (1763) - which ended the Seven Years' War - formally ceded Quebec and Louisiana to Great Britain, but the absence of a nearby French threat to the frontiers of the Thirteen Colonies - as well as the accord reached with the predominantly Roman Catholic French Canadians to preserve their traditions and unique way of life - sowed the seeds of American Independence in the decade which followed.

Red Coat, White Flag

The Battles of Saratoga, September 19 - October 17, 1777

After his withdrawal from besieged Boston, the charismatic Major General John Burgoyne petitioned the government for an overland excursion from Canada towards Maj Gen William Howe's British garrison in New York. The problem was that British authority only extended as far as the shadow cast by a grenadier's mitre and so this bold move would detach New England - the rebellious colonies of Connecticut, Rhode Island, Massachusetts Bay, and New Hampshire - from the middle colonies and allow the British Army to snuff out the American Revolution in its treasonous heartland.

The plan went awry before Burgoyne had even set foot in Canada. Howe, who kept his own counsel to the frustration of his peers, had decided to conduct an operation to capture Philadelphia, the seat of the Continental Congress. In his defence, neither Burgoyne nor the government had made it explicit that Howe was expected to support the expedition from Canada.

Nonetheless, Burgoyne was effectively on his own for what had been sold to the government as a grand pincer movement.

The Northern Department of the Continental Army no doubt felt similarly isolated. The bulk of the force under General George Washington was wintering in New Jersey after countering Howe's breakout the previous year, and so the vital task of keeping Burgoyne from closing his hands around the revolution's neck fell the gouty Maj Gen Philip Schuyler. ➤➤

BELOW: 'Surrender of General Burgoyne' by John Trumbull, 1822. In the centre of the image, Major General John Burgoyne offers his sword to Major General Horatio Gates, commander of the Northern Department of the Continental Army. In white is Colonel Daniel Morgan of the Provisional Rifle Corps.

ABOVE: A hand-coloured engraving from 1798 showing the colonial militia gathering to resist the British at the Battle of Lexington.

The uniquely rugged and self-sufficient character of Britain's North American colonies had been sorely tested by the events of the mid-18th century. The threat posed by both the French and Native American communities hostile to the expansion of the settlers had necessitated British protection, with the colonial governments - noisy, raucous, and staunchly democratic - begrudgingly paying for it.

With the conclusion of the French and Indian War (1754–1763), much of the French threat to the northern and southernmost boundaries of the Thirteen Colonies had been all but obliterated, but Great Britain had been left with enormous debts. The Stamp Act of 1765 was a wide-reaching tax on all printed or published matter, but despite their role in dragging the motherland into war in the first place (see page 12), opposition to the policy of direct taxation resulted in such widespread protest, disorder and even violence - including the tarring and feathering of stamp agents - that the British government relented.

The question as to whether the British government had the right to impose taxes upon its North American subjects was, in the mind of British ministers at least, unquestionably in the affirmative. The point was forced by a series of related legislation called the Townshend Acts, which were passed in Summer 1767, and imposed taxes on an enormous array of British exports to the Americas The colonists, especially those in Boston, capital of Massachusetts Bay Colony, responded with a boycott of British goods and a document which outlined the principles of their opposition. The British Parliament responded with a show of strength, dispatching 2,000 troops to Boston. Rather than quell unrest, the 'lobsters' (as they were derisively named) were seen as an army of occupation and a confrontation between a mob which hurled abuse as well as chunks of ice and a company of panicked British infantry resulted in what is remembered as the Boston Massacre (March 5, 1770), a horrible incident in which five colonists were shot and killed. Again, the contentious legislation was repealed but one tax remained on the books - the tax on tea.

Smuggling was so rife that the tariffs on tea were effectively moot, until the British government was forced to throw the East India Company a bone. Tea was usually purchased in London by licensed agents who would then sell it into markets elsewhere, but the company was struggling financially and so the government allowed them to sell direct, allowing them to take the profits usually claimed by the agents. In order to incentivise the purchase of East India Company tea, the Royal Navy began a massive clampdown on smuggling. With a bounty traditionally paid out to crews for boats and illicit cargo seized, the navy went about their policing duties with a cloth-headed zeal that hardened resistance. On December 16, 1773, at the Boston Tea Party, a mob of protestors threw 340 crates of tea into the harbour at a cost to the troubled East India Company of nearly £2 million in modern money. In response, the Coercive Acts of 1774, which colonists referred to as the Intolerable Acts, dismissed the Massachusetts government and closed Boston harbour. The colony was now on the brink of armed rebellion and the newly installed military governor attempted to impound the stores of gunpowder used by the Massachusetts colonial militia. The militia refused to give ground and the Battles of Lexington and Concord (April 19, 1775) - the first action of the American Revolutionary War - ended with the British fleeing back to Boston and militias from Massachusetts and the neighbouring colonies of New Hampshire, Rhode Island, and Connecticut converging on the city and putting it to siege. From the militia was drafted a regular soldiery called the Continental Army, under the command of General George Washington, and after a series of bitter battles over Massachusetts it was clear there was no turning back and no hope of reconciliation and on July 4, 1776, the United States Declaration of Independence was signed.

Forced to abandon Boston to the Continental Army, the British affected a successful landing at Long Island, where the islands and estuaries gave them the advantage of naval superiority, and they used New York as their beachhead from which to press on into New Jersey and mount maritime operations up and down the coast.

Through Forts and Frontiers

Burgoyne sailed into Quebec to much fanfare on May 6, 1777, and set about mustering a force of 8,600, although fewer than half (3,700) were regular British infantry. Of the rest, 3,000 were German mercenaries, mostly 'Brunswickers' from the Duchy of Brunswick-Wolfenbuttel which was linked to King George III of Great Britain by marriage. There were also 650 Loyalist militiamen, 600 allied Iroquois warriors, and an intimidating train of 138 artillery pieces.

From the northern tip of Lake Champlain which connects the modern Province of Quebec to the State of Vermont, the army sailed to the partly destroyed Fort Crown Point. Despite its disrepair, its guns covered both the rapids linking Lake Champlain to Lake George and the point where Lake Champlain narrowed before continuing through the Hudson Valley and into the colony of New York.

Burgoyne took Fort Crown Point without a shot being fired, the rebels melting away before the distant campfires and the Siege of Fort Ticonderoga (July 2 - July 6, 1777) likewise ended without the roar of a single cannon. Under the cover of darkness, the defenders dispatched their wounded and a guard of 600 men on shallow-bottomed boats down to Skenesboro (now Whitehall, a village in New York State) at the southernmost end of Lake Champlain. Then, the remaining troops made haste for Hubbardton, 24 miles to the southeast through the scorching summer sun.

Brigadier General Simon Fraser and an eager advance party of 850 forged on ahead and collided with the 1,000-strong rebel rearguard at the Battle of Hubbardton (July 7, 1777), whilst Burgoyne - with the wind at his back - pursued and scattered the floating hospital of wounded. The next insurgent redoubt to fall was Fort

ABOVE: John Burgoyne, painted by Joshua Reynolds in 1766 during the Seven Years' War in which he earned a reputation as a cavalry commander and rose to brigadier general.

ABOVE: A later portrait of Horatio Gates wearing the medal he was awarded by Congress for his victory at Saratoga. Oil on canvas by Gilbert Stuart, circa 1793.

Anne after a fierce fight between a British advance party and the 15th Massachusetts Regiment at the Battle of Fort Anne (July 8, 1777) a desperate attempt by Schuyler to buy his Northern Department time to consolidate a defence instead of headlong flight through the woods and mountains. Spooked by a British officer who imitated the whoops and cries of the Iroquois as he ran towards the fighting, the 15th Massachusetts withdrew. As they retreated, they set the timbers of Fort Anne alight, and raced to Fort Edward.

From here, both Burgoyne and Schuyler focused their efforts on transforming the growing British triumph into a disaster. Burgoyne had become somewhat distracted in chasing the Continental Army out of its chain of stockades, and he had long since departed from the original riverine route that would take him into the Hudson Valley. Rather than retrace his steps to Lake Champlain and cross into Lake George, he decided to continue his current heading through the backwoods and took the rough road which followed the winding Wood

Creek - and crossed it as many as 40 times - through a narrow valley of darkened pine.

Off the Beaten Track

That the rebels had taken this path less travelled without much difficulty should not have encouraged him. To begin with, the Continental Army were not dragging an immense, rattling train of supply wagons and artillery. Secondly, Schuyler, whose family ties went back three generations to the very beginnings of Dutch settlement in Albany, knew the country well. He ensured the rugged New England hinterland was turned against the invader. The creek was blocked by fallen trees, artfully tangled against each other to make their removal as difficult as possible, whilst the long bridges bisecting the deep gorges and ravines had been torn down in part or whole.

Burgoyne's column reached the abandoned Fort Edward on July 30 after a punishing three-week trek through the wilderness that had depleted the British provisions and forced the exhausted army to widen roads, drain swamps, and build bridges as they forced their way through the tangle at a mile a day.

In the interim, Schuyler had received reinforcements to bring his strength close to 4,500 and he had undertaken a scorched earth policy to deny Burgoyne crops and shelter around Fort Edward. The loss of the crucial forts on which the Continental Congress had pinned its hopes of closing the frontier with British-held Canada had irreparably done for Schuyler's career. That these relics had no chance of being held against artillery and the British ships prowling the lakes was moot with politicians so far removed from the battlefield that their convictions were rooted in fantasy.

The controversial figure of Maj Gen Horatio Gates - who had connived and failed to replace Washington as the Continental Army's overall commander-in-chief in 1776 - was appointed commander of the Northern Department and on August 19 he arrived at the camp on the River Hudson to take charge.

Meanwhile the British desperately ranged over the landscape in search of forage and supplies, only to find that Schuyler's slash and burn strategy was waiting for them. It was during one of these expeditions deep into neighbouring Vermont that a party of elite Brunswick Dragoons and British light infantry stumbled into a fiercely contested engagement with one of the freewheeling rebel warlords which the American Revolutionary War seems to have produced in abundance. The grizzled Maj Gen John Stark and his 1,800-strong New Hampshire militia had ignored Schuyler's

ABOVE: **A contemporary illustration showing the wide variety of American uniforms, with a militia man on the right and a member of a rifle company on the left.**

orders to retire, and he set about the horseless cavalrymen at the Battle of Bennington (August 16, 1777). A relief party joined the fight just as it was winding down before they too were rolled over by Stark. Almost 1,000 of Burgoyne's men had been killed, captured or wounded - the Brunswick Dragoons were all but wiped out and most of the demoralised Iroquois lost their stomach for the fight, shouldered their packs and began the trek back to Canada.

The Fight for Freeman's Farm

Gates now had perhaps as many as 7,000 men at his disposal and he advanced from Albany to Bemis Heights, a wooded plateau north of the village of Stillwater, where he dug in. He enhanced its natural fortifications - slopes of dense pine, maple and oak veined by ravines which emptied into the River Hudson - with a breastwork almost a mile long, enclosed on its flanks and protected by an artillery redoubt on each face.

Burgoyne crossed the Hudson ten miles north of Bemis Heights and camped at Saratoga, the site of the eventual surrender but not of the two battles that bear its name. His army advanced cautiously in three columns. So many of his allied Native American contingent had deserted that Burgoyne was almost completely without scouts to lead them through the scrub. He blindly advanced to within four miles of Bemis Heights before the rebels revealed themselves, a patrol attacking one of his forage parties who were digging up potatoes in the plot of an abandoned farm. The First Battle of Saratoga (September 19, 1777) - also known as the Battle of Freeman's Farm - immediately revealed the vulnerability of Burgoyne's three columns as they moved over the heavily wooded terrain. While the Brunswickers on the left continued south along the bank of the Hudson towards Bemis Heights, Fraser on the right and Burgoyne in the centre advanced along the road west from Sword's Farm, with Burgoyne turning off ➤➤

Major General John Stark urges his untested militia on to 'Dragoon Redoubt', where a small number of Brunswickers and British light infantry fight on against overwhelming odds.

Major General Horatio Gates watches the First Battle of Saratoga unfold from the high ground.

first just before Freeman's Farm where he had to skirt around a sheer ravine. Fraser had a largely uninterrupted passage along the road and turned north on the far side of Freeman's Farm, well to the front of Burgoyne.

Fraser's target was the high ground to the immediate east of Bemis Heights, which would expose the patriot redoubt to British artillery, but the gap between the British right and centre had widened so much in the passage around Freeman's Farm that he was now dangerously exposed. The hard-fighting rebel rifleman, Colonel Daniel Morgan advanced with the 1st New Hampshire Regiment and his handpicked Provisional Rifle Corps. Suddenly charging from the treeline, the New Hampshires shattered Fraser's grenadiers with a close-range volley, whilst the riflemen fired into the flanks.

With Fraser reeling, Brig Gen Benedict Arnold pushed into the gap between the British right and centre, throwing more and more men at Burgoyne's column as it emerged from behind the farm. The British guns attached to the centre were lost and retaken so many times that 36 of the 48 artillerymen were later counted amongst the wounded. Despite Arnold's hammering, the British refused to crumble. Gates sent no more men forward, continuing to hold them back on Bemis Heights on a purely defensive posture. The battle could possibly have been won there and then had Gates the judgement to support Arnold and Morgan, the two most instinctive and aggressive of his commanders.

Finally, the indefatigable Maj Gen Baron Friedrich Riedesel who had been leading the Germans on the British left and meeting little resistance, swerved to the right and suddenly burst through the trees and onto a nearby hill where he could bathe Arnold's flank in a hail of musketry and grapeshot.

By nightfall, the British held the field but at the cost of 600 casualties. It did not feel like much of a victory, but Burgoyne clung to one slender thread of hope. A letter had arrived from Maj Gen Sir Henry Clinton - left holding New York whilst Howe attacked Philadelphia - advising him that he planned to advance from New York with a small force,

ABOVE: An engraving showing the rebel redoubts on Bemis Heights.

which he hoped would force Gates to fling reinforcements south.

It did not. Although Clinton caused Gates sleepless nights, the passage of time had proven to be the ally of revolution. His army grew as more militiamen arrived clutching hand-me-down firelocks, bringing his strength up to 11,000. Arnold, who blamed Gates for not backing his gambit, was additionally incensed when his commander reported to Congress on the battle without any reference to Arnold's initiative in the attack (or Morgan's success, for that matter). Eventually, Gates tired of Arnold's sniping and divested him of the Continental Army's left flank in favour of the newly arrived Maj Gen Benjamin Lincoln.

Burgoyne dug in around Freeman's Farm. His numbers were diminishing through sickness and desertion, neither scenario helped by the increasingly meagre rations of salt pork and flour, and daily harassment from rebel skirmishers. Winter was now well on its way and without hope of reinforcement or resupply, the Second Battle of Saratoga (October 7, 1777) - or the Battle of Bemis Heights - was one final throw of the dice for not just his 5,000-man command, but the British pacification of the Thirteen Colonies.

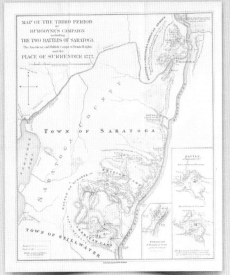

ABOVE: A map of the First and Second Battle of Saratoga, also showing the final positions of both armies at the time of the surrender.

The Last Chance

Burgoyne poised to throw everything at Gates's left flank. Despite their grimy, malnourished shape, the 1,500-strong light infantry under Fraser formed up into its neat lines on a wheat field west of Freeman's Farm, positioned its guns and waited, whilst Burgoyne hung back

with the rest of the army and held his breath. As far as they could see - which was not far through the dense foliage - there was no movement from the rebels.

Again, Morgan was first forward, his riflemen creeping through the woods to Fraser's right, whilst another brigade advanced soundlessly to his left. Behind to Fraser's left, Reidesel's Germans held the centre and another brigade of patriot infantry moved to pin them down. Outgunned and outflanked, the British right crumpled and wavered. With neither Gates nor Lincoln showing any sign of motion, Arnold ignored his orders and gathering a reserve brigade behind him, galloped into the heart of the battle to urge the attackers on. When Fraser was shot in the gut by one of Morgan's sharpshooters, the British right crumbled. True to his martial tradition, Riedesel held his Brunswickers firm as all about them collapsed into chaos, their tattered blue tunics still amongst the disappearing red. For lack of any word to the contrary, the Germans fought on, driving back repeated charges from the militia until Burgoyne's order of retreat made it through the scrum.

The enemy in disarray, Arnold urged them forward and they poured into the British redoubts, pressing on through force of ➤

"Outgunned and outflanked, the British right crumpled and wavered..."

BELOW: Major General Benedict Arnold is shot in the leg leading the rebel charge on the British positions. A copy of a painting by Alonzo Chappel, 1858.

ABOVE: A suitably melodramatic French engraving of the surrender of Burgoyne to Gates, 1780.

numbers. Arnold fell, shot in the thigh but by then the British defeat was complete and only the waning light spared Burgoyne's broken force from being completely slaughtered. Of Fraser's grenadiers and light infantry, 894 were killed, wounded, or captured, depriving Burgoyne of his most valiant commander and over half of the men he had counted on to deliver victory.

By night, the British withdrew - leaving the wounded behind them - and far too late Burgoyne decided to make for Fort Ticonderoga. Now trapped by winter and harassed by skirmishers, he was forced to dig in around Saratoga. With men deserting daily, Burgoyne became indecisive and the army began to disintegrate. Finally, Burgoyne opened negotiations and on October 17, Gates allowed Burgoyne and what was left of his army to be fed, watered and sail for England on the condition they did not return to North America.

Turn to the East

The American Revolutionary War was not even half-way through by the time Burgoyne surrendered at Saratoga, but it was the moment that truly changed the war's outcome. The defeat of the British Army on the field of battle by the rebels showed that they were able to pursue - and triumph - in a conventional war, not just a guerrilla war. This was crucial for enlisting the support of the Kingdom of France, who until this point had been cautious about

tying themselves too tightly to the cause of American independence. A formal alliance was signed in 1778 to supply the rebels with arms, aid and men, and France - aided by its Spanish ally - opened up fronts with Britain in North America, the Caribbean, the Indian subcontinent, and on the open waves. This situation reversed the circumstances of the French and Indian War in which France had been forced to prioritise theatres elsewhere. This time it was Great Britain which was forced to concentrate on the defence of its

ABOVE: A French cartoon mocking Burgoyne's surrender, depicting him as a turkey with his boot in a trap.

profitable Caribbean colonies and the war for the Thirteen Colonies would receive no more reinforcements. With French aid - particularly in terms of naval power and artillery support - the Continental Army was increasingly able fight the British Army on its own terms, as well continuing to fight as it had done in irregular engagements. All hope of Britain being able to salvage some form of victory died at Saratoga, arguably the very second that Howe and Burgoyne's strategies diverged, but certainly by the time Burgoyne pressed on into increasingly hostile territory with inadequate supplies.

In 1783, Great Britain was forced to concede the independence of the United States of America and drawn the war to a close, allowing loyalists to settle in Canada where significant numbers of royalists exiled from the 13 Colonies began to slowly transform the character of what had been until the last decade, New France.

With no possibility for expansion in North America, Britain turned its attentions elsewhere, growing its presence in India where the East India Company was becoming the dominant colonial influence, and settling the southeastern corner of Australia with convict labour in 1787. Defeat in the American Revolutionary War marked the end of what historians call the first British Empire, and the birth of the second, which would grow and endure through the coming 19th century and well into the 20th.

A PHOTOGRAPHIC GUIDE TO THE BATTLE OF BRITAIN'S SURVIVING AIRCRAFT

The Battle of Britain is widely considered to be Britain's finest hour. The 'Few' will not be forgotten, nor will they be around forever to recount the heroism of the summer of 1940 first-hand. In contrast, the number of restored and preserved aircraft in our museums and skies is at an all-time high.

This book features a brief history of all the front-line RAF fighter aircraft that were involved in the famous battle and explores some of the major training and support aeroplanes that contributed to the iconic events. The story is told using over 150 photographs of surviving and restored aircraft in the air, on the ground and in unique formations together.

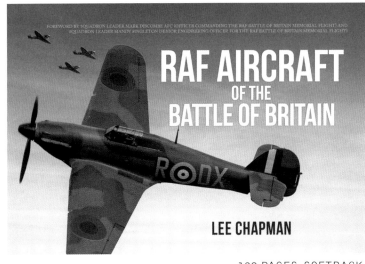

FOREWORD BY SQUADRON LEADER MARK DISCOMBE AFC (OFFICER COMMANDING THE RAF BATTLE OF BRITAIN MEMORIAL FLIGHT) AND SQUADRON LEADER MANDY SINGLETON (SENIOR ENGINEERING OFFICER FOR THE RAF BATTLE OF BRITAIN MEMORIAL FLIGHT)

RAF AIRCRAFT OF THE BATTLE OF BRITAIN

LEE CHAPMAN

128 PAGES, SOFTBACK.

AUTHOR LEE CHAPMAN

Foreword by the Officer Commanding and the Senior Engineering Officer of the RAF Battle of Britain Memorial Flight.

The Tiger of Mysore

The Siege of Seringapatam, April 5 - May 4, 1799

Small and round, with a jet-black moustache, Tipu Sultan neither embodied the warlike tyrant of the Georgian imagination, nor the freedom fighter of later nationalism, but in his deeds, he managed to inspire both. Styled the 'Tiger of Mysore', he kept six of the immense predators chained in his ancient fortress capital, Seringapatam (now Srirangapatna), and adorned everything from matchlocks to the armour of his guards with engraved tiger stripes and fearsome snarling maws. His most prized conversation piece was a musical automaton in the shape of a Bengal Tiger mauling a hapless officer of the East India Company, the best known in a gruesome set showing colonial interlopers being set upon by wildlife.

As the French Revolutionary Wars (1792-1802) upset the old empires of Europe, Tipu Sultan courted the friendship of the new regime in Paris. He opened an embassy, dubbed himself 'Citoyen Tipu' (Citizen Tipu), and draped the Tricolore from the ramparts of his fort. He was an energetic and pragmatic ruler who desperately tried to roll back the British paramountcy in India's economic affairs, but he was also an incredibly cruel one. ➤➤

BELOW: The flag of the East India Company is raised over the battlements of Seringapatam in this 1799 watercolour by Robert Ker Porter.

The aftermath of Carnatic Wars (see page 6) had established the Honourable East India Company as a regional power on the subcontinent, a cuckoo squatting high in the nest of the ailing Mughal Empire. But what had worked in Bengal failed to yield results in southern India, and EIC held only a rump of company territory around Madras.

In all respects, the EIC position in southern India seemed fraught. Not only was their direct control limited, but indirect control - the usual cocktail of coercion, commerce, treaties, and threats - yielded few results. The Sultanate of Mysore had come under the rule of Hyder Ali, its sarvadhikari (chief minister), who siphoned off the power of the Wadiyar maharajas and kept them like peacocks in his gardens. Hyder Ali reformed his army along French lines, purchased modern artillery pieces, and employed rockets fired from iron tubes. He then embarked on a period of territorial expansion which tore chunks off his northern neighbours, the Hyderabad Deccan, and the Maratha Confederacy.

The army of the Madras Presidency was small and they needed local muscle so, in 1766, a triple alliance of the Hyderabadis, the Marathas, and the EIC marched into Mysore as far as Bangalore, before the Nazim of Hyderabad, Asaf Jah II, withdrew - having been bribed by Hyder Ali - and then the Marathas too. Despite some limited successes in the field, without cavalry of their own the British could do little to stop Hyder Ali retaliating by ranging into the Carnatic and up to the very edge of Madras. The First Anglo-Mysore War (1767-1769) ended with the Treaty of Madras (April 4, 1769), a capitulation by the company in which they pledged to come to their foe's aid if Mysore was attacked. When the Marathas invaded in 1771, the East India Company did nothing to oppose them and resentment between the two parties continued to grow. The British defeats in the early stages of the American Revolutionary War (1775–1783) - caused in part by the East India Company's need

TIPPOO SAIB'S TWO SONS deliver'd up to LORD CORNWALLIS, As Hostages, after he had so Gloriously Conquered that Proud Sultan at Seringapatam the Capital of the Mysore Country in the East Indies, in 1792.
Published 23rd Dec 1793 by Robt Sayer & Co. Fleet Street London.

ABOVE: The sons of the Tipu Sultan are surrendered to the East India Company. Mezzotint from 1792.

to sell vast quantities of tea directly into the American market - encouraged France to declare war on its arch-rival in 1780 and they treated India as another front in this global conflict. The EIC had successfully alienated the Nazim of Hyderabad by capturing the French settlement of Mahé which lay firmly within his territory and he was receptive to Hyder Ali's scheme. Emboldened by French support and bolstered with European mercenaries, Hyder Ali invaded the Carnatic again in the Second Anglo-Mysore War (1780-1784), defeated an EIC detachment of 2,800 men and captured Arcot.

Colonel Sir Eyre Coote - a veteran of the Battle of Plassey - was dispatched from Bombay (now Mumbai) and successfully defeated Hyder Ali at the decisive Battles of Porto Novo (July 1, 1781), Pollilur (August 27, 1781), and Sholinghur (September 27, 1781). Now firmly in retreat, Hyder Ali died in December 1782 and his son, Tipu, continued his father's war for a year before agreeing to the Treaty of Mangalore (March 11, 1784), which restored the status quo antebellum but did little to ease the existing tensions between the powers. Tipu - now claiming the title 'sultan' - attacked the neighbouring Raja of Travancore, a company ally which provoked a decisive response from the British. The armies of the EIC, the Maratha Confederacy and the Hyderabad Decca converged on his capital of Seringapatam and forced him to accept the bruising Treaty of Seringapatam (March 18, 1792) which ceded half of his territory to the alliance, including Baramahal, Dindigul, and Malabar to the EIC. He was also forced to surrender two of his three sons as hostages.

HYDER ALLY.

ABOVE: The ruthless Hyder Ali, de facto ruler of the Kingdom of Mysore, by the British artist James Gillray, 1781.

ABOVE: Richard Wellesley, 2nd Earl Mornington, painted between 1813 and 1830 mostly likely whilst he was serving as Lord Lieutenant of Ireland.

he immediately prepared the East India Company for war. First, he had to deal with problems much closer to home. With both the rival Maratha Confederacy and the Kingdom of Mysore employing French instructors to reform their armies, the ruling Nazim of Hyderabad had attempted to secure similar arrangement from Mornington's predecessor but had been rebuffed. This was disastrous for British influence over their fairweather friend, and he promptly employed a French general, Michel Raymond, instead. Raymond established ordnance foundries for cannon, ammunition and small arms, and had soon equipped and trained the entire army of the Hyderabad Deccan in the French style.

Mornington proposed what the Europeans called 'subsidiary alliances', which guaranteed British protection and (almost) complete independence in an Indian state's internal affairs, but in foreign affairs made them entirely dependent on Great Britain.

Although he had substantially increased his holdings at the expense of Mysore during the previous war, the Hyderabad

ABOVE: A very young Colonel Arthur Wellesley, aged 26, and painted by John Hoppner a couple of years before his service in India.

Tipu Sultan's antipathy towards the British met its match in Richard Wellesley, 2nd Earl Mornington and his intense hatred of the French. Mornington - the elder brother of Arthur Wellesley, the future Duke of Wellington - had been appointed governor general of India in 1797 by the British government (the role was in part to curb the excesses of the EIC) and wasted no time in smoking out the perfidious Gallic influence on his doorstep.

Shortly after his arrival in April 1798, Mornington became aware of an alliance being negotiated between Mysore and France - as well as the landing in Egypt of Napoleon Bonaparte - and

BELOW: A flintlock blunderbuss belonging Tipu Sultan and decorated with tiger markings, a hunting scene, and a stylised tiger's head on the flintlock itself.

"Tipu Sultan's antipathy towards the British in Richard Wellesley, 2nd Earl Mornington and his intense hatred of the French."

Deccan was now surrounded by EIC territory or dependencies on almost all sides. With an eye towards the preservation of his kingdom, Nazim Asaf Jah II signed a Subsidiary Alliance Treaty with the Crown on September 1, 1798, and as per its stipulations, he dismissed the French officers from his employ.

Racing Against the Rains

Two armies, one dispatched by the Bombay Presidency - led by General George Harris - and one by the Madras Presidency - led by Lieutenant General James Stuart - marched on Seringapatam. Numbering between 30,000 and 40,000 in total, the vast majority were Indian - only 4,000 were Europeans, including the 33rd Regiment of Foot under Colonel Arthur Wellesley. The third column of 16,000 was made up of French-trained Hyderabadis, dispatched by the loyal Nazim, and according to some accounts still fighting with French instructors.

Restrained by its size and its huge wagon train of elephants and oxen, the pace of the three columns was limited to a maximum of ten miles a day, but they effortlessly swept aside Mysorean resistance. Even a failed night attack by Col Wellesley in the Battle of Sultanpet Tope (April 5-6, 1799) - in which the young officer narrowly escaped capture - was recovered, allowing the British access to Seringapatam where they began to dig in.

ABOVE: Another scene of the battle, this one was produced for the directors of the East India Company and consciously includes the company's sepoys in the fighting.

In most respects, the Siege of Seringapatam proceeded as if it were the technocratic battlefields of Northwestern Europe. Mornington ordered the artillery entrenched to face the western curtain wall of the citadel where his engineers assured him it was weak enough for a potential breach. Surrounded on all sides by the River Kaveri, Tipu Sultan played for time in the hope of delaying the British until monsoon season when the crossing points would be flooded. But despite his procrastination, the siege works continued, and Mornington knew full well he was working to a deadline imposed by the elements. ➤➤

BELOW: Men of the 73rd and 74th (Highland) Regiment of Foot storm the breach in the western wall of Seringapatam. Engraving from 1802.

In a few other ways, the Siege of Seringapatam was like nothing the British had seen before, and the details fascinated and horrified audiences at home. Tipu's rocket troops - arranged into battalions called cushoons - were a formidable psychological weapon as their explosive payloads swept over the British earthworks in an orange arc, but more fearsome yet were the jettis, a subcaste of wrestlers and strongmen who wrung the necks of captured redcoats like hens for the pot, or drove nails into their skulls barehanded.

The Mysoreans fought bitterly to prevent the British digging their earthworks but whilst the batteries north of the river were destroyed, beyond the western walls of Seringapatam, the ground was broken up with scattered groves of cacao palm, abandoned villages, and deep drainage ditches which reduced the efficiency of rockets and raiding parties. Nor were the auguries interpreted by his holy men particularly promising. Though Muslim, Tipu Sultan ruled over a largely Hindu population (not that it seemed to deter him from desecrating the temples and icons of his Hindu enemies), and he attempted to purchase divine favour by showering the Brahmin (priestly caste) with gold, an elephant, two buffalo and all manner of other offerings.

Lion takes the Tiger

By May 2, 1799, the siege works were completed, the artillery opened up and the mine dug beneath the western wall was blown, collapsing the masonry into the river bed. The next day, Major General Sir David Baird ordered in the 73rd and 74th (Highland) Regiment of Foot to secure the opening. Baird, who had fought Tipu Sultan in the previous Siege of Seringapatam (February 5 - March 18, 1792) had a personal stake in taking the citadel. During the Second Anglo-Mysore War 20 years earlier he had been wounded and held prisoner there by Hyder Ali for 44 months. Despite his severe injuries, the musket ball wasn't removed until his release and it's a miracle he escaped death by fatal infection.

With the breach open, it was only a matter of time before the British seized the entire wall. On May 4, at 11am - the hottest part of the day when both armies might be expected to be resting - two columns of 'forlorn hope' were issued a biscuit and a whiskey ration, and splashed through the shallow water of the Kaveri with bamboo ladders. They scaled the walls either side of the breach, followed by a third column of the 33rd Foot to make good on their momentum. According to some accounts, a traitor - the sultan's chief minister, Mir Sadiq, who had kept a line of correspondence with the British without his master's knowledge - withdrew the Mysorean soldiers from the breach under the pretext of distributing their pay. Within 16 minutes, the East India Company standard was fluttering over the ramparts and successive waves of redcoats flooded the inside of the curtain wall.

Tipu Sultan led the defence himself, firing again and again at the invaders with freshly loaded matchlocks handed to him by servants. As the enemy swept the inside of the wall, the 'Tiger of Mysore' was killed in the scrum by an unknown British soldier who stripped him of his jewels and finery. His body was later found in a passageway choked with the dead.

BELOW: An unnamed British officer leads the charge. The sepoys have been pushed to the fringes of the image but the pair in the left foreground - clad in shorts and 'sundial' hats - offer an accurate document of the uniforms worn.

This 1801 engraving shows Tipu Sultan fighting on whilst wounded from the gate of Seringapatam's inner fort.

The Fourth - and final - Anglo-Mysore War ended with the destruction of Mysore as an independent power. The ornamental Wadiyar dynasty was restored to the throne but as clients of the East India Company, giving them control over southern India and factories on both coasts. To much grumbling of nepotism from more qualified men, Mornington appointed his inexperienced younger brother, Col Wellesley, as governor of Mysore.

After Seringapatam, fears of French intrigues in India - no matter how exaggerated they had been - all but vanished and Mornington was free to pursue an openly expansionist agenda. He soon began meddling in the affairs of the Maratha Confederacy which would lead to war with the freshly-promoted, Maj Gen Arthur Wellesley at the helm. Great Britain was no longer merely the dominant European power in India but was quickly becoming the dominant power in India full-stop.

Though the idea of the subsidiary alliances didn't originate with Mornington - or even with the British (the French proposed them first) - in his hands it became a methodical system by which the East India Company and the British government could increase their control over the continent at low cost.

Forbidden from hiring any Americans or Europeans without the company's approval, the client states became closed to outside influence. Not only were they prohibited from raising their own armies, but they had to pay for the privilege of the British garrisons installed for their protection.

The Hyderabad Deccan and the Kingdom of Mysore became the first of what would grow to 565 Princely States. Their rulers were known uniformly as 'princes' despite their actual titles to ensure that they weren't acknowledged as the equal of the British monarch. These archaic principalities cluttered the internal governance of India until they were finally absorbed outright in 1948, their rulers deposed, and their immense wealth confiscated as a casualty of the nation's independence.

ABOVE: Grieving servants present the body of the Tipu Sultan to Major General Sir David Baird. Baird had previously been held captive in Seringapatam by Hyder Ali.

The Unfinished Revolution

The Battle of Queenston Heights, October 13, 1812

In the early 19th century, Canada was divided into three provinces. Upper Canada (much of modern Ontario) clung to the northern shores of the Great Lakes, Lower Canada which stretched from Montreal to the icy Labrador Sea, and the Atlantic Provinces of Newfoundland, Nova Scotia, and New Brunswick.

Whilst Lower Canada was protected from the US by its remoteness and the formidable fortress of Quebec, and the Atlantic Provinces had a more recent population of British-born settlers and geography gave them the protection of the Royal Navy, Upper Canada was predominantly rural, close to the US border, and occupied by settlers born in North America who President James Madison believed were naturally sympathetic to the US and would eagerly grasp the opportunity to rise up against the British.

Although Upper Canada - with its diminutive capital of York (now the city of Toronto) - had barely more than a single battalion of regulars, consisting of the 41st Regiment of Foot, a detachment of retired veterans and an artillery company, Major General Sir Isaac Brock had been preparing for conflict since 1807. Brock, a Guernseyman by birth, considerably strengthened the defences of Quebec, invested in the ➤

BELOW: Major General Sir Isaac Brock breathes his last as the British attempt to retake the artillery redan on Queenston Heights. 1896 chromolithograph by J. D. Kelly.

ABOVE: 'Boney and Maddy', a British cartoon from 1814 of French Emperor Napoleon Bonaparte and US President James Madison 'gone to pot'.

The War of 1812 was a conflict that neither Great Britain nor the United States of America had prepared for. Britain was fighting the Peninsular War (1807–1814) to drive the armies of France from Portugal and Spain, and in part that involved the aggressive search of neutral ships in the Atlantic to prevent them trading with any of Britain's enemies. As one of those enemies until relatively recently (see pages 12 to 24), the US depended a great deal on trade with France.

British subjects, particularly deserters from the Royal Navy, found themselves being impressed for service on British warships where experienced seamen were sorely needed. Service in the Royal Navy - particularly in wartime - was low-paid, dangerous and miserable and many deserters or veteran mariners of British origin had gone on to find far more comfortable positions aboard the large US merchant fleet.

The British believed they were acting entirely legitimately, but many British-born sailors had since been naturalised as US citizens and sometimes suspected innocent men were seized in error, but regardless, few American skippers enjoyed having their crews intimidated and abducted. This flared into violence in 1807 when the captain of the 38-gun frigate USS Chesapeake - who knew he had British deserters on board - refused

Tecumseh and his brother Tenskwatawa personified resistance to US expansion. German print circa-1850.
Library and Archives Canada

Tecumseh und der Prophet.

to allow his ship to be boarded by men from the 50-gun HMS Leopard. In response, Leopard opened fire, killing three of the crew and injuring 18 others. The American surrendered and the British hauled off four deserters, three of which were US citizens.

Coupled with this heavy-handed diplomatic faux pas, the Louisiana Purchase of 1803 which transferred French-claimed territory to Washington, had allowed the US to push deeper into the American interior. An incredible 828,000 square miles of land - including enormous fertile chunks of what is now Arkansas, Missouri, Louisiana, Kansas, Colorado, Wyoming, Iowa, Nebraska, Minnesota, Montana and the Dakotas - was now open for settlement in defiance of the fact they were already occupied. This stirred up indigenous resistance, especially from the Shawnee Confederacy which was caught up in the grip of religious mania under its leader Tecumseh and his brother, Tenskwatawa ('The Prophet'). Eager to sponsor a belligerent buffer state along the vast border with British Canada, Britain supplied arms and aid to the Shawnee.

On June 17, 1812, the United States declared war on Britain citing the trade blockade, the impressment of Americans into the Royal Navy, and the support for the Shawnee Confederacy. Support for the war was limited, especially in the northeastern states of New England, but amongst the hawks were those who latched onto conflict as a means to 'correct' the mistake of the American Revolutionary War - chiefly the failure to count the Canadian colonies as part of the United States.

A posthumous portrait of Sir Isaac Brock by George Theodore Berthon, 1883.

(now Windsor). There he made grand proclamations, encouraging the Canadian militia to throw off the shackles of British tyranny and join them. Despite confirming how lightly defended the way ahead was (Windsor had given no resistance), he was wary of proceeding much further.

Michigan's indigenous population had been less than thrilled to become part of the United States and Tecumseh's Shawnee warriors were already on the move to menace his lines of communication over the frontier. One supply column had been ambushed and slaughtered at the Battle of Brownstown (August 5, 1812), and Hull ordered 600 men detached to re-open the road at the Battle of Maguaga (August 9, 1812). When news of Fort Mackinac's capture arrived, Hull had heard enough and withdrew to Detroit to prepare for the humiliation that would end his career.

Whilst the Americans retreated back across the border, Brock and Tecumseh met for the first time and immediately struck up a rapport, each man impressed by the decisiveness of the other. The Shawnee had captured some of the US Army's correspondence at Brownstown and Brock judged from it that his American counterpart was timid, particularly anxious about being surrounded by hostile Native Americans and feared a long siege of Fort Detroit. On August 16, Tecumseh approached Detroit through the forests with approximately 530 Shawnee and Brock marched down the road towards the fort with around 300 regulars and 400 Canadian militia wearing cast-off uniforms so that the force looked as though it were composed entirely of disciplined British

Provincial Marine which was responsible for military transport and policing the Great Lakes, and built alliances with the indigenous communities. Conventional wisdom on the British, as well as the American side, was that Upper Canada would quickly be overrun and fighting for it was effectively a lost cause, so Brock struck first. He believed that decisive early action would galvanise the defeatist local militia and convince Britain's indigenous allies of their intent, so he sent a scratch force of Native Americans, fur traders, and British infantry to take Fort Mackinac on July 17, 1812. They struck before the American garrison even knew that war had been declared, seizing Mackinac Island, and taking 61 prisoners, and in the process commanding the straits which connected Lake Michigan and Lake Huron.

The Half-Hearted Invasion

On July 12, Brigadier General William Hull - governor of Michigan Territory and commander of the US Army of the Northwest - marched from Detroit and crossed the Canadian border to occupy Sandwich

ABOVE: "The humane British and their worthy allies." A hand-coloured 1812 propaganda cartoon showing a British officer paying a Native American for each bloody scalp he hands over belonging to an US soldier.

ABOVE: Queenston looking towards the heights, painted a few years prior to the War of 1812 by Edward Walsh. Aquatint based on the original watercolour.

line infantry. He had sent ahead a letter which warned Hull: "It is far from my inclination to join in a war of extermination, but you must be aware that the numerous body of Indians who have attached themselves to my troops will be beyond my control the moment the contest commences."

After conjuring up Hull's deepest fears of massacre and mutilation at the hands of the Shawnee, Tecumseh paraded his warriors before the walls, and Brock unleashed a two-hour bombardment on the fort, pounding away at the American commander's already brittle nerves. Although the defenders outnumbered the attackers almost two to one, they were mostly locally-raised militiamen whose thoughts soon turned towards the families they had left behind undefended on their farms. Their commitment to a conflict born out of the intricacies of ocean-going trade policy and dreams of empire-building were limited indeed.

At 10am a white flag waved from the walls and Hull ordered his men lay down their muskets. The British took possession of Fort Detroit, 2,188 prisoners, 39 cannon and a large stock of guns and ammunition. For surrendering the garrison without a fight, Hull was later court martialled for cowardice and sentenced to death, although President Madison pardoned him and let him off with a dismissal.

Brock was all set to continue his advance into Michigan but to his dismay, Lieutenant General Sir George Prévost, governor general of the Canadas, negotiated an armistice with a view to ending the war entirely. News travelled slowly in the early 19th century: two days before the declaration of war, the British government had repealed the 1807 Order in Council that blockaded Europe to American trade and as that was a significant part of President Madison's casus belli, Prévost hoped the whole affair might still be brought to a peaceable conclusion. Madison, however, was committed to war and all the armistice ultimately achieved was to pass the offensive momentum from Britain to the United States.

Slaughter on the Escarpment

Whilst morale in Upper Canada soared as a result of Brock's victory, the general was deeply aware that a harder fight lay ahead, and that the province would not be secure until the Americans had been decisively beaten back. Unsure where the next attack would come once the armistice expired, Brock based himself at Fort George at the town of Niagara-on-the-Lake and scattered his available manpower - roughly 1,500 regulars and militia, and 250 indigenous auxiliaries - along the river which separates Lake Ontario from Lake Eerie and Upper Canada from New York.

In the early hours of October 13, 1812 an invasion force of over 3,000 directed by the wealthy local landowner Maj Gen Stephen van Rensselaer - commander of the US Army of the Centre - began crossing the treacherous rapids to Queenston. The force consisted of 900 regulars of the 6th, 13th and 23rd US Regiments of Infantry and 2,650 men of the 16th, 17th, 18th, 19th and 20th Regiments of New York Militia, but the small peacetime US Army had expanded so rapidly and haphazardly for the War of 1812 that there was little difference in terms of training, motivation or experience between most of the fighting men.

Their destination lay only a few miles north of the thundering Niagara Falls and beneath the town rose the escarpment of Queenston Heights which ran east to west from the water's edge. Sited up on Queenston Heights overlooking the village was a redan, a clifftop artillery emplacement with a single mortar, 18-pdr cannon, and the light company of the 49th Regiment of Foot. A mile north of the village another gun at Vrooman's Point also maintained vigil over the river with a company of the 5th Regiment of Lincoln Militia. The village itself was garrisoned by the grenadier company of the 49th (or the Hertfordshire) Regiment of Foot, a company of 2nd Regiment of York Militia (York Volunteers), and a detachment of the 41st Foot with a light 3-pdr 'grasshopper' cannon. ➤➤

ABOVE: The British garrison at Fort George viewed from its US counterpart Fort Niagara by Edward Walsh.

and the plume of his hat obvious amid the redcoat ranks - a sharpshooter's musket ball struck home and Brock was slain. His aide-de-camp Lieutenant Colonel John MacDonell carried the charge forward to the very edge of the Queenston Heights before he too was wounded, and the British fell back towards Vrooman's Point.

By now reinforcements were on their way from Fort George under the command of Major General Roger Sheaffe - including Cap Robert Runchey's Company of Coloured Men, a unit made up of both slaves and free men - but it would be hours before they entered the fight.

In the chaos of battle Rensselaer had only managed to get around 1,000 men across the Niagara and his demands for the rest to follow fell on increasingly deaf ears. It transpired that the sight and sounds of battle had brought out the barrack room lawyers amongst the New Yorkers, who pointed out that, constitutionally speaking, the New York Militia were only required to serve within New York State, which

Their boats visible even in the darkness, the British fired in opposition with the artillery battery soon chiming in as the invaders paddled furiously towards the shore. On the US side of the Niagara, two 18-pdr guns began to pour shot into Queenston village. Seven miles away at Fort George, Brock was roused from his slumber by the sounds of distant gunfire and without waiting, galloped off towards the battle. Fearing it was a diversion for a larger attack elsewhere, he ordered only a few detachments after him to shore up the British defences.

As the Americans hit the shore, they found themselves dangerously exposed, pinned down by the guns above them on the escarpment. With the sky growing lighter with the approach of dawn, the British artillery became increasingly accurate and the Americans refused to cross, leaving their stricken comrades floundering on the Canadian shore. Only by chance, a

ABOVE: 'Brock's Midnight Gallup' to the battlefield, from the watercolour by Charles W Jeffreys, 1908. Library and Archives Canada

fisherman's path was spotted winding up to the escarpment and Captain John Wool, 13th Infantry, led a charge to capture the redan and silence the guns. From there, the Americans were able to fire down into Queenston's defenders, now suddenly as exposed as their adversaries had been minutes before.

The Empire Strikes Back

Brock arrived at around 5am and realising the scale of the invasion, sent a message back to Major General Roger Sheaffe at Fort George. Realising that the odds were firmly stacked against them, but unwilling to leave the Americans commanding the battlefield whilst more bluecoat reinforcements rowed across the channel, he formed up the two companies of York militia and the two companies of 49th for a desperate assault.

As they climbed the slope to the redan, Brock led the way with his sabre aloft. Picking out his general's uniform - his gleaming buttons

the Province of Upper Canada most certainly wasn't. In frustration, Rensselaer crossed back to try and reason with them.

Back on the Queenston Heights, a party of 80 Mohawk, Haudenosaunee, and Delaware warriors under the command of the Scottish-born half-Cherokee Major John Norton, harried the confused invaders. His brave band raced through the trees on the edge of the escarpment, peppering the Americans with musket balls before disappearing again, whilst Sheaffe took a wide arc from the village and up around the back of the escarpment, keeping well out of range of the American cannon. The Native American war cries from the undergrowth proved as effective here as they had done at Fort Detroit and after having been fighting for over ten hours, the Americans began to panic and falter. At 4pm, Sheaffe was in position. Forming a disciplined line, the British volley was the end of the matter. With nowhere to

ABOVE: A portrait of Major John Norton in the garb of a Mohawk chief by Mather Brown, 1805.

flee and fearful of a Mohawk massacre, 925 survivors surrendered. The Americans had taken an estimated 300 casualties compared to 14 British dead and 77 wounded, and Rensselaer later resigned in disgrace.

The Best of Enemies

Brock's death was keenly felt across the province, but he had left the Canadians with a proud fighting legacy and he had shown that the annexation of Upper Canada to the United States was no foregone conclusion. A new Canadian national identity began to form, hardening their resistance. Although most of the fighting had been undertaken by British regulars and their Native American allies, the vital role played by the citizen-soldiers of the militia was essential in building national pride. More invasions were attempted before the War of 1812 had run its course, but for the most part the Americans were driven back again and again by a people now certain their destiny was distinct to that of their more populous and developed neighbour.

After the penultimate defeat and exile of the French Emperor Napoleon Bonaparte in 1814, Britain committed more resources to its unplanned war with the US, infamously setting the White House ablaze in the process. The Treaty of Ghent (December 24, 1814) simply restored the status quo. President Madison's terms - that Canada be turned over to the US - were completely ignored by his own negotiators who instead put their efforts into resisting British attempts to create a Native American buffer state. Neither party saw their

ABOVE: The road up onto the escarpment taken by Major General Roger Sheaffe and his reinforcements, marked with a stone reading 'Sheaffe's Path to Victory' in this 1913 watercolour by Owen Staples.

more outlandish goals become a reality and ultimately it was North America's original inhabitants who suffered the most from the peace. Tecumseh was killed in battle in 1813, the Shawnee Confederacy was crushed, and their lands seized.

Perhaps the most meaningful outcome was that 1814 marked the beginning of over two centuries of peace - albeit with the odd spat here and there - between Britain and the United States, without which neither great nation would have been able to prosper and grow. The US had failed to achieve any of its war aims, but in winning a number of crucial battles on land and sea, it had established itself as the equal of its old colonial master and over the next few decades Great Britain largely refrained from antagonising its prodigal son.

BELOW: James B. Dennis's early 19th century oil painting shows the American troops crossing the River Niagara and seizing control of the Queenston Heights.

Although Napoleon Bonaparte had brought the Prussians to their knees at Ligny, he declined to finish them off. Complacent that they were now a spent force, the French emperor decided to go after Wellington, who had retreated north towards an excellent defensive position, the gentle Mont-Saint-Jean escarpment that he had previously discovered near the village of Waterloo.

To have the best chance of beating the French, Wellington required the assistance of the Prussians under Generalfeldmarschall Gebhard Leberecht von Blücher, but he was still unable to contact them. In the meantime, he gazed out over the French camp through his telescope - they were unnerving still despite the previous day's bloody set-to at the Battle of Quatre Bras (June 16, 1815). As the army began to mobilise as discreetly as they could to avoid giving the French warning of their intentions, a Prussian officer rode into camp with a report about the battle at Ligny and his army's subsequent retreat towards Wavre.

In the French lines, Marshal Michel Ney had also been waiting anxiously for news of the Battle of Ligny (June 16, 1815). His priority was to prevent the British and Prussian armies linking up and so in the absence of instruction from Bonaparte he had decided to avoid spooking Wellington with an early morning offensive. In Ney's opinion, the best course of action would be for he and Bonaparte to combine forces as quickly as possible and take Wellington on before the Prussians were able to regroup, however as the hours rolled by, the emperor failed to make an appearance.

Instead, as the Prussians regrouped at Wavre and Blücher, who had been seriously injured at Ligny, recovered, Bonaparte ordered his men to set up camp and wasted most of the following morning enjoying a late breakfast and then a tour of the previous day's battlefield. Like Ney, he believed that the best policy would be to attack Wellington, but by the time he had ➤

The Grave of an Empire

The Battle of Waterloo, June 18, 1815

BELOW: The smoking, casualty-strewn field of Waterloo, the morning after the climactic battle that decided the fate of Europe.

The Battle in Context

ABOVE: 'The 28th Regiment at Quatre Bras' by the celebrated Victorian military artist Elizabeth Butler Thompson shows French cavalry assailing a British infantry square, 1875.

France had long been Great Britain's principal rival, but the French Revolution (1789-1799) unsettled the balance of power on an enormous scale. The French Revolutionary Wars (1792-97) gave way to the Napoleonic Wars (1803–1815) with the rise of Napoleon Bonaparte as the self-proclaimed Emperor of France. This series of on-off conflicts consumed much of Europe and inevitably spilt over into European empires across the globe, resulting in the Fourth Anglo-Mysore War (see page 26) and the War of 1812 (see page 32). Alliances shifted as nations alternately fell under French influence, or wiggled free, and in 1807 Great Britain was forced to confront its greatest fear: a protracted land campaign in Europe without reliable (and preferably German) allies.

The Peninsular War (1807–1814) was a wicked learning curve for the small professional British Army, but under the command of Arthur Wellesley - who rose from major general to field marshal, and from baronet to Duke of Wellington during the campaign - and with variable degrees of support from the bitterly divided Spanish, they managed to drive the French from Portugal and Spain, and push on into southern France. Elsewhere - emboldened by British success in Iberia - Prussia, Russia, and Austria, plus a host of the smaller German states - had crawled out from under their humiliating accords with Bonaparte. By early 1814 the French found themselves fighting to defend Paris from a coalition consisting of half the European continent and the nation's survival depended on offering up its emperor. Finding even his loyal marshals had given up on him, Napoleon Bonaparte abdicated and went into exile on the island of Elba, only 12 miles off the coast of Italy.

Thanks to his sympathisers who kept him informed of events at home, he knew that the new Bourbon king, Louis XVIII and his court, whose restoration had initially been met with much enthusiasm, were already well on their way to becoming as unpopular as Louis XVI and his court had been before the French Revolution. Most importantly, the soldiers of the French army especially disliked Louis XVIII. On February 26, 1815, just over nine months after he had first arrived there, Bonaparte escaped from Elba, taking with him the small force of 700 men that he had managed to muster on the island. With every town he passed through on the mainland, more French soldiers joined his cause, including the marshals who had thrown him to lions so eagerly just a year before.

The victorious nations of 1814 had pledged to complete their victory, promising scores of troops to send Bonaparte packing. Wellington and his Prussian counterpart, Generalfeldmarschall Gebhard Leberecht von Blücher mustered their forces in Belgium and waited for the Austrians and Russians to mobilise in turn.

Bonaparte was not going to give them the chance. After fighting a war on multiple fronts over the last decade, he intended to snuff out each rival in turn. He moved quickly into Belgium in order to come between the two allied armies and prevent them joining forces. The Prussians were trounced at the Battle of Ligny (June 16, 1815) and Blücher was seriously injured, whilst the British just about clung on at the Battle of Quatre Bras (also June 16, 1815) and spent the night camped within earshot of the day's bitter opponents.

AN IMPERIAL VOMIT.

ABOVE: In this 1814 print, King George VI of Great Britain holds a peace treaty behind the back of the vomiting Bonaparte as all the nations of Europe tumble from the Emperor's mouth.

ABOVE: Marshal Michel Ney, with his shock of red hair, leads a charge later in the battle. From a larger painting by French expressionist Louis Dumoulin.

Blücher from nearby Wavre pledging the support of not just two corps of Prussians, but his entire army. Wellington expected the Prussians to form up on the left of the battlefield as it was closest to Wavre and so moved his own troops into the right and centre. He also fortified the Hougoumont estate on the right and the hamlet of Papelotte on the left to protect their flanks.

The following morning, Wellington was up early to inspect his troops. He had 68,000 men under his command, predominantly British, supported by the Dutch and some of the smaller German states. The French army, which amounted to 73,000 men, had taken up position on a ridge to the south but lacked line of sight on Wellington's army and knew that the fortifications at Hougoumont and Papelotte made his flanks difficult to turn.

ordered the marshal into action, most of the allied troops were slipping away and Ney was forced to send a large force of French cuirassiers to harass the British rearguard. The resulting rolling skirmishes between the British and French cavalry were made more perilous by a terrible thunderstorm and torrential rain.

Bonaparte was now convinced that the defeated Prussians would be limping towards Namur and Liege and sent the right wing of his army, which was headed by Marshal Emmanuel de Grouchy, Marquis de Grouchy, in pursuit while holding back the left wing and reserves for his confrontation with Wellington. It was not until late that night that Grouchy realised that the Prussians

were in fact on their way north to Wavre. The marshal prevaricated, before eventually sending a message to the emperor that he intended to give chase, but by which time there was no hope of catching them up.

Drawing the Battle Lines

By the end of the June 17, Wellington and his men were safely ensconced on Mont-Saint-Jean and busily setting up camp for the night. As he had hoped, they had been able to take up position in the shelter of a long ridge where he could use the reverse slope to conceal his strength, as he had done to great effect so many times in the Peninsular War (1807–1814). As Wellington surveyed his lines, he was heartened by a message sent by

BELOW: Wellington and his staff watch from Mont-Saint-Jean as the Battle of Waterloo unfolds around them in a great panorama.

ABOVE: Lieutenant General Henry Paget, Marquess of Anglesey, and Earl of Uxbridge (in red) leads the 7th (Queen's Own) Light Dragoons (Hussars) into French infantry in this watercolour by Charles Turner Warren, 1823.

At 6am, while Wellington was surveying the field at Waterloo, Blücher was at Wavre, overseeing a flank march of his troops, which would be led by the Prussian IV Corps. However, a mixture of exhaustion, sodden roads from the previous evening's heavy rain and a fire that closed several streets slowed their progress, and the last men finally cleared Wavre six hours after the Prussian army began its manoeuvre. Meanwhile, Bonaparte dismissed the idea that the Prussians would be able to join the battle, insisting that they would need more time to recover from Ligny and that Grouchy was more than able to mop them up at Wavre. Determined to follow his commander's order to the letter, Grouchy rejected the advice of his subordinates who told him that as most of the Prussians were already on the move it would be better to head them off at Waterloo. Instead, he made his way to Wavre with

33,000 men only to find all that remained was the 17,000-strong Prussian III Corps, which had been ordered to linger at Wavre and prevent Grouchy from being able to affect the outcome of the Battle of Waterloo.

The Gates of Hougoumont

At Waterloo, the rain had stopped but Bonaparte decided to delay the onset of the battle in hope the ground would dry out and allow him full use of his cavalry. Finally, after several hours of tense waiting on both sides, he began his offensive with an attack on the fortified British post at Hougoumont.

The fighting at Hougoumont was bitter and would last for several hours with the French managing to get past the defence to attack the troops massed on the British right. Although it has been suggested that Bonaparte used his attack upon Hougoumont as a means of diverting

Wellington's attention away from other areas of the field, it is clear that both men believed that holding Hougoumont was key to victory. Meanwhile, Bonaparte ordered that the 80-gun Grande Batterie begin their bombardment of the enemy centre - although with limited success thanks to Wellington's positioning of his men on the far side of the slope.

It was at 1pm in the afternoon, shortly after the cannons began their bombardment that Bonaparte noticed the arrival of increasingly large numbers of Prussian soldiers - the advance parties of Blücher's force. Chagrined by this unwelcome sight, he fired off a message to Grouchy, demanding that he leave Wavre and instead bring his men to Waterloo to cut down the Prussians as they arrived. Grouchy did not receive this missive until the evening, by which time he had already decided ➤➤

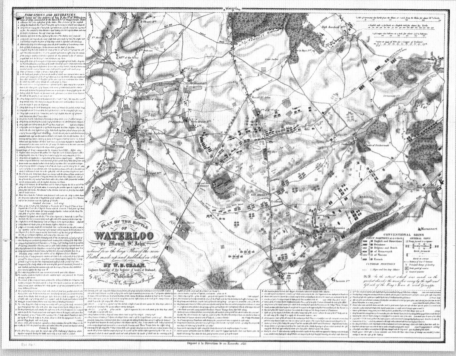

ABOVE: An incredibly detailed 1845 map of the Battle of Waterloo, well worth studying in detail.

to attack the Prussian corps that had been left behind at Wavre. A pyrrhic victory as the larger French force easily defeated the Prussians, but by then the Battle of Waterloo had already been decided.

In the wake of the punishing bombardment, the French infantry advanced in large columns. With the weight of their greater numbers, these unstoppable battering rams of men and muskets pushed the British troops before them, breaking their lines and scattering them.

Within an hour, it very much looked as though Bonaparte was winning and Wellington's situation had become perilous. Blücher's men had been arriving in a steady stream since midday, but by 3pm they were still too few to turn the tide.

Desperate to regain the upper hand, Wellington's dashing cavalry commander Lieutenant General Henry Paget, Earl of Uxbridge brought the Household Brigade and the Union Brigade out of their concealment behind the ridge and sent them into the fray to assist their beleaguered infantry colleagues. The Household Brigade charged down the embankment and swept through the enemy, scattering the French cuirassiers who were defending their left flank and then crashing through the French infantry. However, they went too far into the field and found themselves in trouble until the Union Brigade, so named because it comprised cavalry regiments from England, Wales, Scotland, and Ireland, came to their rescue.

In the ensuing fighting, the 2nd or Royal North British Dragoons - popularly known as the 'Scots Greys' - captured the treasured eagle standard of the 45th Ligne, one of the leading French regiments, while the 1st (Royal) Dragoons captured that of the 105th. Despite the elegance of a cavalry charge, it is in effect nothing more than a guided stampede and once started was in danger of overshooting or running out of momentum. This had happened to the Household Brigade earlier and would now happen to the intrepid Union Brigade, who found themselves in the midst of the enemy and with little clear idea what to do next In the fighting that ensued

"Within an hour, it very much looked as though Bonaparte was winning..."

BELOW: Uxbridge leads the Household Brigade into the French cuirassiers, by the Victorian military artist Orlando Norie, 1870.

The 2nd or Royal North British Dragoons - better known as the Scots Greys - make their decisive charge in this watercolour by Orlando Norie, 1880.

the Scots Greys were virtually wiped out and the rest of the British cavalry suffered heavy losses. However, they had bought the British line crucial time to regroup and restore its disciplined lines.

The Squares Stand Alone

While the cavalry slashed their way through the French foot, Wellington ordered the casualties moved behind the lines and out of the range of enemy guns. Observing this movement from his own vantage point, Ney mistook the distant movement as a general retreat and decided to take advantage by pressing home with another attack. With most of his infantry either caught up in the abortive attack on Hougoumont or scattered by the British cavalry, his own cavalry was the only card he had left to play. The first charge, which involved 4,800 cuirassiers and a light cavalry division of the Imperial Guard, was easily repulsed by Wellington's infantry, which responded by forming dense squares, four ranks deep, which stood their ground behind a thicket of bayonets. The artillery took refuge within the squares as the French cavalry attacked and then unleashed a blazing firestorm on the attacking horse. Having sacrificed his light cavalry on the altar of opportunity, Ney sent in an additional 9,000 men, including the heavy cavalry corps. His cavalry commander General François Christophe de Kellermann quickly realised that the enterprise was doomed to failure and so did his best to keep his most elite regiments from the field, only to be overruled by Ney.

Though the advance of the French heavy cavalry was an impressive sight, it failed to make much impression upon the British who stood firm within their disciplined formations. The infantry square was effective against cavalry, but against artillery and infantry it was little more than a tightly-packed shooting gallery where each strike of French flint against black powder could not help but draw blood. Finally, Ney ordered another full infantry attack combined with

more cavalry charges and a heavy artillery bombardment.

At the same time, General Jean-Baptiste Drouet, Comte d'Erlon's troops were attacking La Haye Sainte, a walled farmhouse in a crucial position at the bottom of the escarpment. It had been heavily fortified and garrisoned by 400 German and British troops but at around 4pm, the defenders ran out of ammunition. The French seized control shortly afterwards and used it to ➤➤

ABOVE: This apocalyptic 1816 print shows the desperate fight for the farm at Hougoumont, which anchored the British flank.

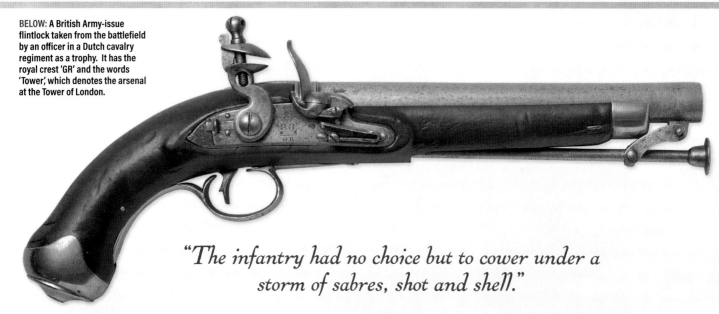

BELOW: A British Army-issue flintlock taken from the battlefield by an officer in a Dutch cavalry regiment as a trophy. It has the royal crest 'GR' and the words 'Tower', which denotes the arsenal at the Tower of London.

"The infantry had no choice but to cower under a storm of sabres, shot and shell."

move men and artillery within 60 yards of Wellington's centre, which they proceeded to bombard at short range with canister shells which scattered a murderous crown of shrapnel over the redcoats.

While the artillery pulverised the British centre, multitudes of French light infantrymen, called tirailleurs, poured into La Haye Sainte and began to fire upon the squares, which were unable to retaliate in strength whilst French cavalry continued to swarm. They even fired at Wellington and his staff when they rode too close to the farmhouse, causing them to flee through a nearby hedgerow and Wellington to seek safety in the heart of a square. The British

situation was now looking hopeless - they were unable to take back La Haye Sainte, their cavalry was spent, and the infantry had no choice but to cower under a storm of sabres, shot and shell.

Wellington and Blücher had agreed earlier that if the British centre was under attack then the Prussian should attack Plancenoit, which was ideally placed to act as a conduit to the French rear. General Georges Mouton, Comte de Lobau was sent to intercept the small number of engaged Prussians before they reached Plancenoit, but his troops were forced out of the way by a lethal bayonet charge. Without reinforcements, they were quickly driven out again by the French

reserves. Meanwhile, the Prussian I Corps, led by General Hans Ernst Karl, Graf von Zieten had arrived on the battlefield to support Wellington's left, much to the dismay of the French who had hoped to see Grouchy and the delight of the British who began to push back against their tormentors.

Wellington's centre was still dangerously exposed and at 7.30pm, Bonaparte decided that it was time to deploy his veteran Imperial Guard, which had never been defeated in combat. The Imperial Guard nearly punched a hole in the British line until they were thrown back by Dutch forces led by Lieutenant General David Hendrik Chassé at which point other regiments moved in for the

ABOVE: A highland regiment forms a square and braces itself for the oncoming French cuirassiers and lancers by William Heath, 1836.

ABOVE: A melodramatic German depiction of Napoleon leaving the battlefield as his army fights on, making his way through the rear echelons of wounded and prisoners.

kill, eventually forcing the French to retreat. When the news spread through the French ranks that the great Imperial Guard, the pride of their army, had been forced to retreat there was a tremendous uproar only to be swiftly cut off as Wellington, triumphantly raised himself on his stirrups, waved his hat in the air and ordered a general advance on the confused and fleeing French.

The moment was made all the sweeter by the fact that after hours of intense fighting, the Prussians had just managed to storm and seize Plancenoit and gain access to the French rear. Although Bonaparte had been confident of victory, he had nonetheless stationed two battalions of the Old Guard nearby to either act as a final reserve or, in the case of defeat, his bodyguard.

Seeing the battle turn into a confusing and shambolic melee, he now made a final attempt to rally his army behind these two elite battalions but to no avail as his left, right and centre were all smashed beyond repair and his armies were forced to retreat, surrounded by the straggling, shell-shocked and devastated survivors.

A New World Order

That evening, as darkness fell upon the torn and ravaged battlefield, which was littered with thousands of dead and dying, Wellington and Blücher met for the first time that day and saluted each other. Their victory over the French was complete but had come at a high cost to both sides with a total of 24,000 men on the allied side killed, injured or missing in action while the French lost 41,000, including the 6,000 men who were captured during the retreat.

A handful of desultory skirmishes followed before Bonaparte accepted defeat and abdicated for the second time. Refusing to make the same mistake as they had in 1814, he was exiled to the infinitely more remote South Atlantic island of Saint Helena, a British colony with a newly installed garrison, where he would die in 1821. For Europe, the decisive defeat of Napoleonic France meant a reshaping of the balance of power and the emergency of new regional powers, including Prussia which would go on to displace Austria as the north star of the German-speaking world and led ultimately to German unification.

Diplomacy and disputes over the next century would be guided by the peace of 1815 and the need to maintain a balance between the so-called Great Powers of France, Prussia, Russia, Great Britain, and Austria. The precariousness of this plate-spinning act would be tested numerous times before it finally shattered in 1914, but for the most part the great nations of Europe contented themselves with the business of colonialism, commerce and snuffing out the nationalist aspirations that the spirit of Bonaparte had left simmering across the stateless peoples of Latin America, Eastern Europe and the Balkans.

The Congress of Vienna, which prematurely outlined the post-Napoleonic settlement in 1814, was primarily concerned with the borders and political composition of Europe, but the defeat of France had consequences too for the British Empire. All signatories condemned the slave trade, increasingly at the heart of Britain's conversion to moral as well as merchant superpower, and British ownership of a number of strategically crucial new territories was confirmed. These included former Dutch colonies of Ceylon (now Sri Lanka) and Cape Colony, from where the fruits of the British Empire in southern Africa would blossom, and Tobago in the Caribbean. Plus, the French Indian Ocean islands of Mauritius and Seychelles, the Caribbean island of Saint Lucia, and the eastern Mediterranean stronghold of Malta. Britain additionally gained a protectorate over the Ionian Islands, part of what is now Greece.

Betrayed and Butchered

The Battle of Gandamak, January 13, 1842

The British had discovered for the first time that invading Afghanistan is far easier than conquering it. The garrison in Kabul was trapped and although there were reinforcements at Gandamak - five days' march away - the road between was covered with guerrillas. Meanwhile, the garrison at Kandahar was five weeks away at least and that was assuming that snow had not closed the mountain passes. The British camp, or cantonment, was vulnerable in the extreme. Rather than occupy the ancient citadel of Bala Hissar, some surplus of confidence had situated their encampment in low-lying marshy ground overlooked by surrounding hills, and its stores were held in a separate compound which was soon overrun. Attempts to drive the Afghan fighters from the nearby village of Bemaru or to silence the artillery on Bemaru Heights ended in disaster, or at best, only temporary respite from the constant sniping.

By November 16, 1841 news reached the weary cantonment that reinforcements had left Gandamak, but they were not coming to the relief of Kabul. Their commander, in defiance of his orders, had deemed a rescue mission suicide and instead was withdrawing to Jalalabad, 80 miles east of Kabul and on the edge of the Khyber Pass.

The recently appointed commander of the British forces in Afghanistan, Major General Sir William Elphinstone, was a kindly man, but not a particularly impressive one. Pushing 60 and crippled with rheumatic gout, he had not seen action since the Battle of Waterloo, and he looked to the veteran civil servant Sir William Hay Macnaghten to bring events to a close. ➤➤

BELOW: 'The Last Stand of the 44th Regiment at Gundamuck, 1842' by William Barnes Wollen, 1898.

The Battle in Context

ABOVE: Tribesmen watching over the Khyber Pass by Captain Lockyer Willis Hart, 1843.

Whilst Britain's mercurial East India Company increased its holdings in Bengal and along the eastern coast of the Indian subcontinent (see page 6) at the expense of the waning Mughal Empire, the fractious Pashtun tribes banded together. With the disintegration of Persia's Safavid Empire in 1736, the former Safavid cavalry commander Ahmad Shah Durrani realised that only the threat of war bound the Pashtuns together. He pushed north to consolidate much of what is now Afghanistan and then south into Mughal lands from Kashmir to Karachi.

Durrani had built an empire but not a state. The business of his succession led to almost 50 years of in-fighting that saw no less than seven monarchs take the throne before stability came with the wily Dost Mohammad Khan. Piece-by-piece the southern frontiers of Ahmed Shah's domain had been consumed from below by the aggressive new Sikh Empire of Maharaja Ranjit Singh, the 'Lion of Punjab'. The Sikh army - the Dal Khalsa - seized the bulk of Ahmed Shah's conquests south of the Khyber Pass, the strategically vital mountain choke point through which armies had entered the subcontinent from the days of Alexander the Great. The loss most keenly felt was that of Peshawar, a wealthy city in the heart of a fertile province.

Meanwhile, Russia and Great Britain had become fixated on a shadow war that the British dubbed 'the Great Game'. Russian designs - which also contributed to the outbreak of the Crimean War (see page 60) - were to gain a warm water port. British anxieties coalesced around not only having a rival at sea but of the unlikely spectacle of the Russian army marching down the Khyber Pass and into India.

With an eye to the recovery of Peshawar, Dost Mohammad attempted to play the two imperial powers off against one another. After being refused an alliance with the British who were more afraid of antagonising the Sikhs, he courted a Russian diplomat in the hope that it would lead to a better offer from the British. Rather than give Dost Mohammed a stronger bargaining position, he had inflamed British anxieties to the point of hysteria. In December 1838, an army of 10,000 British and East India Company troops and 6,000 supporters of the exiled former king Shuja Shah Durrani marched on Afghanistan. Taking the long way round rather than the heavily defended Khyber Pass, they met with little resistance. By August 1839, Kabul was in British hands and in 1840, Dost Mohammad surrendered himself to palatial exile in India (the very same palace vacated by Shuja Shah Durrani). He was playing a long game.

Shuja Shah was not a popular ruler. His first order of business had been to formally cede the disputed frontier to the Sikhs before levying punitive taxes on the peasants. Meanwhile the British were losing money at the same pace the king was acquiring it: the new government in London baulked at the expense of the occupation and they began to withdraw troops and cut off the subsidies paid to the Ghilji (or Ghilzai) tribe to keep the passes open. Banditry and violence surged and then in November 1841, a mob stormed the British Residency in Kabul, murdering its occupants who they found entertaining local women. The capital was now in revolt with the British - soldiers, sepoys, and civilians - besieged in their cantonment a mile outside the city, and the unwelcome king skulking in the ancient fort of Bala Hissar.

ABOVE: Emir Dost Muhammed Khan sought British aid for his war with the Sikh Empire.

Into the Wild

Elphinstone had no choice other than to assume that Muhammed Akbar spoke for all Afghans, but he was not a unifying figure like his father. He was from the Durrani (named after the traditional ruling dynasty) and he had no control over the rival Ghilji tribe who held the passes to the east. Nonetheless, Muhammed Akbar took several officers and their wives as hostages, to ensure that the British would abide by the terms of their agreement. Not that there was anything to ensure that he would do likewise.

With only five days-worth of provisions and no Pashtun escort, on January 6, 1842, 4,500 troops and 12,000 camp followers set off along the perilously winding road through the snow-capped mountains of the Hindu Kush. Even without an enemy, the danger of the elements was enough as sub-zero temperatures cloaked the ravines and slopes with deep snow. The majority of the column, military and civilian, were Indian and most had never experienced a climate so cold. They slept with snow on their feet and by the first morning a dozen had died from exposure, whilst frostbite had tightened its grip on many more. Within days, Elphinstone would relate that few of his sepoys retained enough fingers to fire their muskets. As they marched, many sepoys simply dropped their weapons and fell back to join the mass of civilian camp followers - families, labourers, servants, merchants, and other vital parts of an army on the march. Some simply gave up and sat themselves down by the side of the road to await death. It was not long in coming. Throughout the day, nimble Afghan horsemen harassed the vanguard, cutting down those who fell behind, making off with the baggage, and sowing panic amongst the camp followers. On January 8, they approached the first of

ABOVE: A British East India Company column marching through a mountain pass in considerably nicer weather.
Wellcome Collection CC BY 4.0

In November, Muhammed Akbar Khan - son of the exiled emir Dost Muhammed - arrived in Kabul. An experienced military commander who had been waging a guerrilla war in the highlands, Macnaghten thought he had found someone with whom he could do business. On December 11, dwindling rations forced Macnaghten to agree with Muhammed Akbar and the tribal chiefs for the British to vacate Afghanistan entirely, an extraordinary concession made out of sheer desperation. They would be allowed to buy provisions for their journey and be given an escort by Muhammed Akbar which would guarantee safe passage to Jalalabad.

The chiefs agreed and although Muhammed Akbar was paid handsomely by Macnaghten, the supplies failed to materialise, and their departure date constantly shifted without explanation. Scheming furiously to find an escape from their predicament, Macnaghten gleaned that some of the chiefs weren't entirely thrilled with the idea of the father being restored to the throne and he reached out to them, promising that if they wanted the British to remain in Afghanistan he would have no hesitancy in breaking his agreement with the son. On December 23, 1841, Macnaghten was summoned to another meeting with the chiefs and murdered in full view of the cantonment. Whilst the horrified defenders watched his body stripped of clothes and valuables, the stunned Elphinstone refused to act or to sanction retaliation. Now alone, he had no choice but to wait for their departure date, provisions, and escort to materialise.

ABOVE: 65th Bengal Native Infantry circa 1846 by Henry Martens. By the 1820s, sepoy uniforms followed a similar pattern to regular British infantry with shakos and white cross belts.

an oasis emerging from the desert, this was all illusionary but at this point, Elphinstone had no option but to pay and pray. He had stopped giving orders entirely and just shivered in his saddle, following the flow of beleaguered bodies. On January 9, the princeling offered to take all the women and children hostage so that they would be under his protection. Though his promises so far counted for nothing, Elphinstone had reason to hope that this would be different - the Pashtun honour code (Pashtunwali) put much stock in the granting of sanctuary to those who threw themselves on a chieftain's mercy.

On January 10, the survivors passed through the narrow Tunghi Taraki Gorge - said to be so deep that the sun never touched the floor - where the press of rock forced them into single file and boulders joined the musket balls which met them from above. Those who faltered or cowered in cover were finished off later with a long Persian-style knife called a pesh-kabz, a symbol of manhood amongst the hill tribes. Now only 240 soldiers and 3,000 of the camp followers remained of those who had set out from Kabul mere days before. ➤➤

the narrow routes through the Hindu Kush, the foreboding five-mile Khurd-Kabul Pass. There the Ghilji had prepared low stone breastworks from where they could pick off the defenceless mass below. They wielded intricately decorated hand-made long rifles called jezails, far higher calibre than the British 'Brown Bess' muskets and with a far greater range, they allowed the Ghilji to pepper the British at a great distance and leaving them with no hope of returning fire.

Within days snow blindness joined frostbite and exposure as opponents just as bitter as the tribesmen who filled the air above them like carrion birds. At regular intervals, Muhammed Akbar popped up to demand further concessions and take more hostages, promising that supplies lay just ahead. Like

ABOVE: The British column is ambushed high in the Hindu Kush in this illustration from The Romance of Empire by Victor Surridge (1909).

RIGHT: Pashtun tribesmen with a jezail long rifle, depicted in 1848 by James Rattray. The purpose of the idiosyncratic curved stock is unknown, but possibly so it can balance in the crook of the arm when on horseback.

A later view over Jagdalak where Major General Sir William Elphinstone's army disintegrated, by James Rattray, 1848.

ABOVE: A 19th-century Afghan pesh-kabz, a long stabbing knife of Persian origin.

Pass of Thorns

Unable to stomach another terrible assault, they decided to make for the next pass by night and slip through under the cover of darkness. As they crept towards the two-mile-long Jagdalak Pass, distant gunfire spooked the camp followers who immediately surged through the infantry throwing the column into chaos. As cold light began to break over the jagged peaks, they could see in their mind's eye the Ghilji taking up their positions, their jezails balanced on the rocks, and their knives sharpened. They rested in the village of Jagdalak itself, ominously quiet although its walls offered some protection and respite for the vanguard who had been fighting off attackers all morning. With the morale of the sepoys having disintegrated, Elphinstone was only able to depend upon the 44th (or East Essex) Regiment of Foot, the only British regulars in his force. Whilst the miserable column rested, Muahmmed Akbar summoned Elphinstone and his second-in-command, Brigadier General John Shelton of the East Essex, to negotiate their safe passage through the Jagdalak Pass with the chiefs of the Ghilji. Now, recipients of the prince's hospitality, the two officers were fed and slept by the fire, before spending the next morning fruitlessly listening to chieftains howl abuse and promise the many ways in which they would butcher the infidel. In the distance,

they heard the guns begin to bark as Brig Gen Thomas Anquetil had assumed the worst of his commander's disappearance and was fighting through the pass. Meeting a tangle of holly oak at the narrowest part of the road, those who tried to scale the six-foot abatis were shot and the tribesmen closed in to finish off their cornered prey. Some escaped in the chaos, slipping through the blockade, but Anquetil was slain.

Elphinstone, a better gentleman than general, demanded to be allowed to rejoin his men, but he was informed that he was now a hostage to ensure the safe return of the exile Dost Muhammed Khan. It is probable, that was the plan all along.

All ordered retreat had now broken down completely and in the frosty morning light of January 13, a small group of 20 officers and 45 infantrymen, mostly from the 44th left the road to take up positions on a small hill near to the village of Gandamak. They were down to no more than two or three musket cartridges per man, whilst the officers drew their swords and revolvers, but the hill at least gave them a fighting chance against the Pashtun horsemen. Once the last shot had been fired, they fixed bayonets and charged.

A few miles away another group - around a dozen mounted soldiers, mostly from the 5th Bengal Light Cavalry - gallop wearily into the village of Fatehabad where the

locals offered them yoghurt and bread. Few received the dignity of dying in battle. As they dismounted, they discovered the serpent had beaten them to Eden and were set about with clubs and swords. The only survivor was Assistant Surgeon William Brydon, Indian Medical Service, who had the fortune to stuff a magazine in his hat for warmth which absorbed the killing energy of the blow. He managed to mount up and gallop off.

The Army of Retribution

Whatever the British garrison at Jalalabad had expected to see, it was not a single beaten man on a dying horse. When asked what had happened to the army, Brydon replied: "I am the army."

Of course, Brydon was not the only survivor although mythology often describes him as such. Thousands of sepoys and civilians made their way to the slave markets of Central Asia or limped back to Kabul where they lived as maimed and frostbitten beggars, while a few drifted into Jalalabad in the days following Brydon's race to safety. Gravely ill with dysentery and despair on top of his existing ailments, Maj Gen Elphinstone died in captivity, although the hostages were well treated and 115 survived to see freedom. In that doughty Victorian fashion, an attempt was made to conjure up the tragic heroism of the retreat from Kabul, but there is no escaping the enormity of the tragedy. The mountainous northwest that marked the very limit of British influence in India never lost its malevolent reputation.

ABOVE: The face and reverse of what is usually known as the 'Candahar, Ghuznee, Cabul Medal' for service in the 1842 Army of Retribution.

The humiliation of the retreat from Kabul shattered the myth of inevitability that had grown around the British conquest in India, sowing the seeds of the Indian Mutiny of 1857 (see page 68). It should have also sounded a warning note too, that the East India Company policy of replacing inconvenient rulers with more pliant ones has its limits. Left high and dry by his British patrons, Shuja Shah attempted to switch sides and after emerging from his fortress hideaway, he was murdered, and Muhammed Akbar Khan declared himself emir.

More immediately, Britain needed to deal with Afghanistan in a way that restored national pride but did not leave them repeating the errors of 1841. In summer 1842, two armies advanced from Kandahar and Jalalabad, under the direction of Major General George Pollock who had forced his way through the Khyber Pass at the head of an 'Army of Retribution'. Kabul was retaken in September 1842, Muhammed Akbar Khan was defeated, a few buildings were destroyed, and the hostages were released. Less than a month later the British returned to India as if some great undertaking had been concluded as opposed to thousands of lives lost in terrible agony and fear for no strategic gain. In 1843, Dost Muhammad Shah returned to Afghanistan and life carried on as normal.

> "*The mountainous northwest that marked the very limit of British influence in India never lost its malevolent reputation.*"

'Remnants of an Army' by Elizabeth Butler, 1879, showing Assistant Surgeon William Brydon arriving in Jalalabad.

Crushing the Khalsa

The Battle of Aliwal, January 28, 1846

With the news that Dal Khalsa, the increasingly unpredictable army of the Sikh Empire, was advancing towards the British supply lines at Ludhiana, Lieutenant General Sir Hugh Gough detached a force to send them packing. Gough, who loved a spot of shock and awe, had summoned a siege train from Delhi and the thought of the Sikhs stumbling across his heavy artillery on the road did not bear thinking about.

Like his CO, Major General Sir Harry Smith had seen action at the Battle of Waterloo (June 18, 1815) and had distinguished himself in the various colonial campaigns of the 1830s. Though his relationship with Gough was poor, his skill as a commander was undeniable and he was tasked with protecting the army's lines of communication.

Moving swiftly, Smith recaptured the forts at Fatehgarh and Dharmkot, before advancing towards Ludhiana. He was reinforced en route by the British Army's prestigious 16th (the Queen's) Light Dragoons (Lancers), 53rd (or Shropshire) Regiment of Foot, and by the Bengal Army's Colonel Godby with two regiments of Bengal Native Infantry and two battalions of Gurkhas, hard-fighting Nepalese soldiers. Smith's numbers were now close to 10,000 men, with 32 guns.

The Sikh column under Ranjodh Singh Majithia was still following the river towards Ludhiana at a disarmingly casual pace. Majithia's force consisted mainly of irregulars, ill-disciplined levies in contrast to the steely Sikh regulars of Dal Khalsa, and despite having a head start and the benefit of following the road, Smith's column arrived into Ludhiana on January 21 exhausted and dehydrated from the forced march through the heat of summer. It was normal practice for the army to march by the cooler air of the night and rest through the day, but Smith drove his men relentlessly, hoping to come between the Sikhs and Ludhiana. ➤➤

BELOW: The 16th (the Queen's) Light Dragoons (Lancers) - the only British cavalry regiment with a red, rather than blue tunic - charge through the Sikh guns and into the infantry triangle. Interestingly, the uniform of Dal Khalsa also consisted of a red tunic. Painting by Orlando Norie, 1846.

The Battle in Context

Pakistan. All of this the Sikhs viewed with suspicion, although from the British perspective they were merely strengthening their frontiers against a militarily powerful but unstable neighbour. However, there were factions within the colonial administration who saw the political intrigues within Punjab as an opportunity to increase British dominion and seize the wealthy Sikh Empire. Meanwhile, the Sikh court - the Durbar - gleefully led the sabre-ratting, gambling that a war would cut down the influence of Dal Khalsa. On December 11, 1845, the First Anglo-Sikh War began as Dal Khalsa crossed the Sutlej and Lieutenant General Sir Hugh Gough, a veteran of Waterloo, marched to meet them. The Sikhs struck first and were pushed back at the Battle of Mudki (December 18, 1845) and then they were driven from their entrenched positions at the Battle of Ferozeshah (December 21-22, 1845), which forced them to withdraw across the Sutlej and back into Punjab. Both generals, Raja Lal Singh and Tej Singh, belonged to the faction at court - one dominated by Hindus of Dogra ethnicity who had converted to Sikhism - opposed to the ascendant Dal Khalsa. Both were accused of leaking information to the British and resigned their positions.

With the apparent traitors replaced and the army reinforced, one column crossed the frontier further north under the command of Ranjodh Singh Majithia and moved towards the British cantonment at Ludhiana in order to menace the British supply lines, whilst another crossed closer to Ferozeshah and established a forward position at Sobraon.

ABOVE: Maharaj Ranjit Singh, founder of the Sikh Empire, circa 1830.

As the East India Company's only credible rival in northern India, the British had trodden carefully to avoid antagonising the highly militarised Sikh Empire, whose army - Dal Khalsa (meaning 'the Pure') - had been organised on European lines. Following the death of their conquering king, Maharaja Ranjit Singh, the Lion of the Punjab, in-fighting consumed the empire and the Sikhs churned through four rulers in three years, before settling on Ranjit Singh's youngest son, the five-year-old Duleep Singh.

With all his predecessors (his brothers) having been murdered or overthrown, the infant maharaja could do little to curb the growing power of Dal Khalsa which had become an increasingly autonomous state-within-a-state. Regiments began to make decisions by panchayats, a council of five representatives elected by the soldiers themselves, which was mirrored at brigade level and by the army command - the system had prevented Dal Khalsa from disintegrating during the empire's power struggles, but it had effectively partitioned the civil and military leadership completely.

The British, meanwhile, had stumbled backwards into ramping up tensions. In 1843, the East India Company annexed Sindh to the south of Punjab, cutting off the Sikh Empire's access to the sea, and established a military cantonment (semi-permanent camp) at Firozpur, on the banks of the Sutlej River which now marks the border between India and

ABOVE: A soldier of the Sikh Empire and his wife by an Indian artist, circa 1840.

ABOVE: An unknown battle in the Second Anglo-Sikh War with the British sepoys on the left and the Sikhs on the right. Wellcome Collection CC BY 4.0

Majithia had grown wary at the news of Smith's progress and rather than push on to his objective, he ducked back across the Sutlej River to gather reinforcements - including some sorely needed regular infantry. The strength of Dal Khalsa was in its infantry and artillery, both trained in the European style but strengthened by the

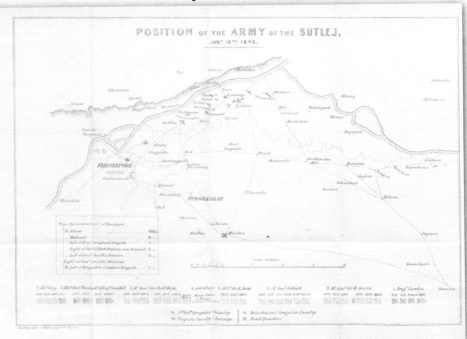

ABOVE: A map of the Sutlej River campaign, showing the fighting in the British controlled east of Punjab.

ABOVE: An 1857 lithograph of Major General Sir Harry Smith, issued following the triumphant Battle of Aliwal.

uniquely martial faith of the Sikhs. Only in terms of cavalry did they leave much to be desired and the Sikhs were forced to rely on gorcharras, mounted feudal levies raised by the rural aristocracy and clad in an archaic lucky dip of armour and weapons. In all, Majithia had around 12,000 men, 2,000 cavalry and 52 artillery pieces.

Hide and Sikh

Smith had expected to fight the Sikhs at Ludhiana, but discovering they had turned north back towards Punjab, he immediately gave chase. Cautious of the superior British cavalry and wishing to lean into his own superiority in cannon, Majithia recrossed the Sutlej with his augmented force and

ABOVE: The Sutlej campaign medal belonging to Corporal Charles Pye, who served in all the major confrontations of the First Anglo-Sikh War with the 31st (or the Huntingdonshire) Regiment of Foot.
© Auckland Museum CC BY

took up a purely defensive position between the villages of Aliwal and Bhundri, with the river at their back beyond a low plain. The Sikh lines were a mile and a half long, with the guns evenly spaced. Majithia placed his most reliable troops on the right flank at Bhundri and a smaller force of regulars on the left at Aliwal. The centre was held by the irregular infantry, the peasant levies who were sheltered by a long ridge, which they entrenched with earthworks.

Perhaps almost entirely fixated on the threat of the British cavalry, Majithia had invested his entire strategy in countering any attempts by the enemy to turn his flanks or to press on his rear. Their only line of retreat was a ford, in front of which the Sikhs had pitched their tents and lit their cooking fires. Maybe he was also gambling that the shaky centre would be forced to hold firm if its only alternative was drowning in the fast-flowing Sutlej.

As the two forces came within sight of one another on January 28, Smith formed up in the typical fashion for the British Army in the middle of the 19th century: two infantry brigades in the first line, two in the second line, and then the cavalry in reserve. As they advanced, the Sikh guns began to roar their opposition and Smith ordered the second line to extend on the right and move on the village of Aliwal, from where they would be able to send volley after volley down the length of the enemy lines.

With the left flank beginning to crumble, Majithia sent in the gorcharras to retake Aliwal. In response, the first of the two British cavalry brigades advanced to flush them out - three regiments of Bengal Light Cavalry (1st, 5th, and the Governor General's Bodyguard) and the dashing Shekhawati Brigade of irregulars, who galloped forward in a cloud of dust. With the gorcharras driven off, the infantry advanced towards the Sikh camp and the ford. As Majithia tried to reform the Sikh lines around Bhundri, he sent the gorcharras into the plain over which the British were now advancing, and once his infantry had been consolidated, they followed. Again, the British cavalry was sent forward - a squadron of the 16th Lancers and 3rd Bengal Light Horse. The 3rd Bengalis baulked at charging a thousand-strong mass of thundering hooves and glittering chainmail, but the 16th Lancers wasted no time wetting their spears and putting to flight a host ten-times their number. The light Sikh horses and their sword-wielding riders were simply unable to match the weight of the heavier chargers or the reach of a cavalry lance.

ABOVE: The young Maharaja Duleep Singh depicted in 1847 at the age of eight.

Dirty Lancing

As the Lancers galloped back to the British lines, they found their route blocked by the Avatabile Regiment, so-called because it was drilled by the Italian mercenary Colonel Paolo Avitabile. The Avatabiles formed a triangle, a variant on the infantry square that ensured any rider who broke through the edge found themselves pinned like a rat in a trap between the blades, bayonets, and barrels of the other two sides. Despite a fearsome volley from the Sikh muskets, the Lancers - supported by the guns of the Bengal Horse Artillery - broke through the Avatabiles but at a cost of 42 of the 100 men killed or injured. ➤➤

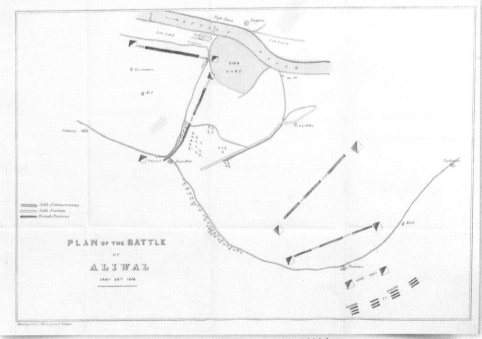

ABOVE: A contemporary map of the Battle of Aliwal, showing the progress of the British forces.

The remaining squadrons of the 16th were then sent forward to silence the Sikh guns, which fired until the very last second before their crews rolled under the carriages to escape the lethal tips of the British spears. With another infantry triangle moving up to block their passage, the 16th had no choice to charge onward, taking a similarly heavy toll as they punched through the bristling mass of Sikh soldiers. Riding back to the gleeful Smith who showered them with praise, those of the 16th able to fight on were formed up into a single unit and pointed in the direction of Bhundri. Followed by a bayonet charge from the 53rd Foot, the 16th took the second village and the Sikhs

began a disorderly flight across the river. A few pockets of Dal Khalsa tried to fight on, with Majithia attempting to form a new line on the opposite bank before the British cannon scattered them across Punjab.

The British counted 141 dead and 413 wounded (the 16th Lancers took a total of 140 casualties out of 300 men). The cost to Dal Khalsa was much higher, with perhaps as many as 3,000 slain.

Divide and Conquer

Regarded as the turning point of the First Anglo-Sikh War, the decisive defeat of Dal Khalsa at Aliwal shattered the illusion of Sikh martial supremacy that cowed many of the sepoys in the Bengal Army. Major General

Sir Harry Smith was later showered in praise and appointed Baron Aliwal, with the victory being described by Arthur Wellesley, Duke of Wellington as tactically perfect, with all arms of Smith's force committed.

Smith rejoined Gough for the Battle of Sobraon (February 10, 1846), a bloody last stand in which many of Dal Khalsa opted to fight for the death rather than give their foe the satisfaction of surrender.

Within days, the capital of Lahore had fallen to Gough and the government negotiated the Treaty of Lahore (March 9, 1846) to bring an end to the fighting. Huge swathes of the frontier, including Kashmir, were transferred to the East India Company in lieu of reparations, the Sikh army was

capped at 20,000 infantry and 12,000 cavalry, and a British Resident was installed in Lahore with sweeping authority to meddle in affairs of government. The regency of the infant maharaja's mother, Maharani Jind Kaur, was replaced by a council, and she was sent into exile with a generous pension.

Hostility to these punitive conditions resulted in an uprising two years later, which expanded into the Second Anglo-Sikh War (1848-1849). Following a crushing defeat at the Battle of Gujrat (February 21, 1849), the ten-year-old Maharaja Daleep Singh was forced to abdicate and sign over his nation to the East India Company.

The defeat of the Sikh Empire represented the last regional rival Great Britain had

in India, but it also resulted in a new relationship between Britain and its former enemies. Despite lingering hostility to the new regime, the Indian Mutiny of 1857 was seen by many Sikhs not as a war of emancipation from a foreign invader, but as an effort to restore the rule of the Islamic Mughal emperor. The tensions between different faiths and ethnic groups in northern India were not lost on the British who saw the wariness many Sikhs felt towards neighbouring Muslims and Hindus as something which could be exploited. The uniquely militant character of their faith and the respect the British afforded the Sikhs as an enemy saw them increasingly sought after for the reconstructed British Indian

Army, especially the Punjab Irregular Force and the elite Corps of Guides, which stood watch on the wild North-West Frontier with Afghanistan.

The 'Martial Races' theory developed to explain why certain communities had remained loyal to the British and others had not. This mix of crude divide-and-conquer, dubious anthropology and pseudo-science posited that certain northern Indian groups - such as the Punjabis, Jats, Rajputs, and Pashtuns (or Pathans) - were naturally better suited to military service, albeit under the direction of white officers, than educated high-caste Hindus whose desire for self-determination was recast as lazy and indolent.

BELOW: Another depiction of the charge of the 16th Lancers through the Sikh artillery.

The Valley of the Shadow of Death

The Battle of Balaklava, October 25, 1854

To the shock of all, over a month after Russia's humiliating withdrawal from the Alma Heights, the vital port of Sevastopol remained in Russian hands. Having squandered their chances of a quick, decisive victory, the British and French were dug in on the southern side of the city in anticipation of a siege.

Prince Alexander Menshikov, the Russian commander-in-chief in Crimea, believed that if they whisked the British Army's supply hub at Balaklava out from under them, the British would either draw men away from the Siege of Sevastopol for a counter attack - giving the defenders breathing space to counter attack themselves - or cut their losses and begin a full withdrawal. Either way, it could end the war before winter set in.

Sevastopol's hinterland was given scant consideration by the British commander, General FitzRoy Somerset, 1st Baron Raglan, who remained focused on the city. The Balaklava Valley, which was divided by the Causeway Heights - a ridge running east to west - curved down to Balaklava in the South Valley, while the Fediukhin Heights jutted out into the North Valley like the prow of a ship.

Six crudely built redoubts clung to Causeway Heights over a mile-long front as a concession to security. Garrisoned by Ottoman troops with British artillery pieces, these inexperienced raw recruits were 'esnan', North African irregulars of mostly Tunisian origin and had been left in their miserable fortifications for days on end without food. Some even complained that they had not been issued the correct ammunition for their muskets. ➤➤

BELOW: A detailed panorama of the Battle of Balaklava from the privileged perspective of Lord Raglan and his staff on Sapouné Heights, a perspective he seemed to forget his men in the field did not share.

The Battle in Context

In the decades following the Napoleonic Wars, Great Britain remained far more likely to go to war with its old enemy across the English Channel than with the Russian Empire of Tsar Nicholas I. In 1830 tensions had flared when France invaded Algeria and old spectres of war of the continent were further revived in 1852 when the French president Charles-Louis Napoleon Bonaparte - nephew of his namesake - declared himself Emperor Napoleon III.

France's attention, however, was not on Great Britain, but Russia. The Russian Empire had been slowly creeping south along both shores of the Black Sea, interfering in the European vassals of the declining Ottoman Empire in the west, and conquering its way through the myriad Muslim states of the Caucasus in the east. Russian eyes were fixed on the need for a warm-water port or at least unrestricted year-round access to the oceans, and on Jerusalem. The tsars had traditionally styled themselves protectors of the Ottoman Empire's Christians, by merit of the Eastern Orthodox church representing the largest single Christian congregation in the Balkans and Near East.

Napoleon III was also interested in Jerusalem. His powerbase depended on appeasing France's deeply conservative Roman Catholics, as well as the French army who approved of a belligerent foreign policy. With inflammatory rhetoric being projected by both patrons, the Catholic and Orthodox communities of the Holy Land began to squabble over ownership and access to the Christian sites. After France took control of a number of shrines, Tsar Nicholas I despatched an envoy to Istanbul to demand that he be given custody of the Ottoman Empire's 12 million Orthodox subjects, effectively giving Russia carte blanche to meddle in the internal affairs of Turkey.

Great Britain was alarmed by both the idea of growing Russian sea power, but also by the disintegration of Ottoman authority which was viewed as vital to the balance of power. Emboldened by French and British assurances, the Ottoman sultan rejected the Russian ultimatum and in response the Russians occupied the Danubian Principalities of Moldavia and Wallachia (parts of modern Romania), with the intention of driving on towards Constantinople (now Istanbul). French and British fleets were dispatched, entering the Black Sea to support the Ottoman navy. The Crimean War, although it did not yet have much to do with Crimea, had begun.

The hastily-formed Army of the East arrived in all its pomp for the largest British overseas engagement since the Napoleonic Wars. It was an army that had for the most part gone unchanged since 1815 and a senior staff who learned their trade at the side of the Duke of Wellington. The 65-year-old British commander in chief, General FitzRoy Somerset, 1st Baron Raglan, was so institutionalised that he habitually referred to the enemy as 'the French'. They eventually landed at Varna on the Black Sea coast of Bulgaria with the intention of supporting the Ottoman offensive to retake the Danubian Principalities, when the Russians abruptly withdrew.

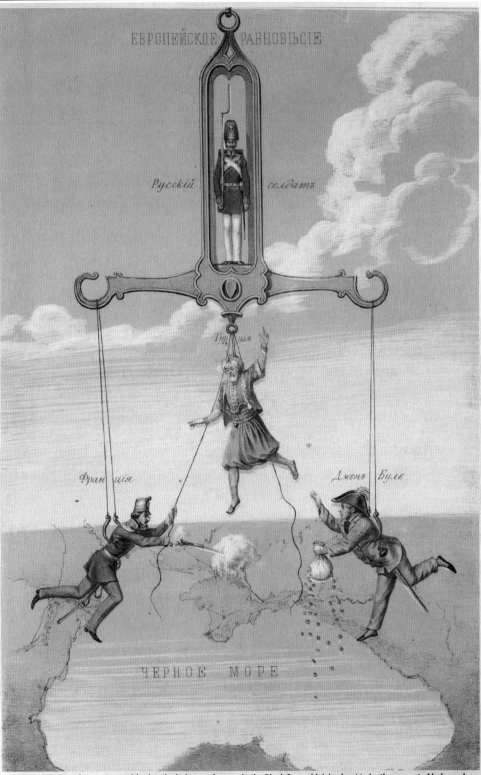

ABOVE: An 1853 Russian cartoon critiquing the balance of power in the Black Sea, which is about to be thrown out of balance by French belligerence on the left and British greed on the right.

In an egregious example of mission creep, the allies decided to deploy their armies on the Crimean Peninsula - itself detached from Ottoman influence in 1784 - and capture the naval base at Sevastopol, the key to Russian maritime power in the Black Sea.

Although unprepared for a long campaign, or even a winter campaign, the allies landed in Crimea on September 14, 1854 and pushed the Russians back towards the city, driving them from their last line of defence before Sevastopol itself at the Battle of Alma (September 20, 1854).

'Lord Raglan' by Roger Fenton. Prior to being assigned command of the Army of the East, Raglan was Master-General of the Ordnance. He had never led a large force in the field.

Highlanders High and Dry

At first light on October 25, the Russians advanced. The redoubts sounded the alarm while the Russians chased Lucan's pickets from the village of Kamara at the eastern end of Causeway Heights and installed their artillery. For hours, the Kamara battery hammered No. 1 Redoubt, the easternmost strongpoint in the chain.

Reacting quickly, Campbell pulled the 93rd Highlanders back towards the village of Kadikoi, where they could shelter from the Russian guns in a patch of dead ground behind the crest of a hill. Lucan drew the Light Brigade back to camp to act as a reserve and ordered the Heavy Brigade into the South Valley hoping to deter the Russians with a show of readiness.

Pressured from the north by advancing Russian infantry and from the east by Russian cannon, the beleaguered Ottoman defenders held out until 7.30am, fighting ferociously despite their miserable conditions and the disdain in which they were held by their allies, before breaking.

Lord Raglan had been roused from his tent as soon as the guns began to bark. He dithered at first, worried that the attack was a diversion, and arrived just in time to witness the Ottoman retreat from the redoubts. From his vantage point on Sapouné Heights, 600 feet above the Balaklava plain at the western end of the battlefield, Raglan was painfully aware of how vulnerable the British supply lines had become. He urgently ordered up the 1st and 4th Divisions and pulled back the Cavalry Division so that they could consolidate with the reinforcements.

Raglan had ordered the 1st Division to proceed directly across the plain into the

Behind the redoubts on the South Valley was the 93rd (Sutherland Highlanders) Regiment of Foot and their commander, the Highland Brigade's heroic Major General Sir Colin Campbell. The Cavalry Brigade were stationed to the Highlanders' right - frequently sending out patrols between Balaklava and the River Tchernaya - and a final line of some 1,000 Royal Marine Light Infantry held the heights above the port itself. The cavalry was increasingly spoiling for a fight. Having played little role in the war so far, they were dismissively referred to as 'look-ons' - a pun on their commander, Lieutenant General George Bingham, 3rd Earl of Lucan - by the infantry. For the cavalry, the war so far had been behind the lines with Lucan feuding incessantly with his second in command and brother in law Lieutenant General James Brudenell, 7th Earl of Cardigan, a toxic dynamic which had resulted in frosty silence. Neither Cardigan nor Lucan could exchange a civil word with the other and all communication was done by proxy.

Supplies dock at Balaklava's Cossack Bay in 1855, taken by James Robertson.

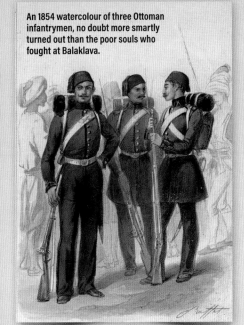

An 1854 watercolour of three Ottoman infantrymen, no doubt more smartly turned out than the poor souls who fought at Balaklava.

93rd's left flank, perhaps intending for the 4th Division to move down into the redoubts from the west. The second half of the order was never spoken, and its commander assumed he was also to advance into the plain.

BELOW: The view from the mouth of Balaklava harbour, packed with British ships, by photographer James Robertson, 1855

Meanwhile, Campbell ordered the 100 walking-wounded of the Invalid Battalion - men reduced to 'light duties' around camp - to occupy a patch of high ground in front of Kadikoi. The 1,100 Ottoman soldiers who had successfully rallied also formed up behind Campbell's battalion. They were expected to be of little help and the 93rd (Sutherland Highlanders) Regiment of Foot would bear the brunt of the Russian advance alone. The Russian cavalry rode along the North Valley behind the captured redoubts and turned to face the Highlanders, 400 of them peeling off to charge.

Rather than form up into the traditional square or four lines to resist cavalry, Campbell had the men arranged into two lines to present the maximum possible number of rifles towards the foe. As he had the Highlanders, Campbell arranged the Ottomans into two lines to receive the charge but as the enemy neared, they fled. At 1,000 yards the accurate new Minié rifles of the 93rd Highlanders thundered in a wicked chorus, following with a second and then third volley which sent the Russian cavalry reeling, circling back to their lines.

Suitably chastised, a larger detachment of 2,000 cavalry and Cossack outriders now swept down over the Causeway Heights towards the 93rd. Suddenly realising that he had left the Highlanders dangerously exposed and that the Ottomans were showing signs of turning tail, Raglan had ordered the bulk of the Heavy Brigade back into the field and suddenly the 700 dragoons of the Heavy Brigade emerged as if from nowhere. Spotting the tips of the Russian lances over the hill, they wheeled left and charged the enemy flank at 100 yards. In amongst each other in an instant, the colliding cavalry formations were so tightly packed that the Highlanders could see little save the flash of plunging steel. Despite the benefit of their greater numbers, the enemy broke and retreated to the North Valley and the protection of the Fediukhin Heights, where the watching Russian guns turned back the cavalry's pursuit.

As the Russian momentum faltered, the British 1st Division and 4th Division arrived on the plain alongside the French 1st Division and two squadrons of the elite Chasseurs d'Afrique light cavalry. The threat to the vital supply hub at Balaklava had been ended, and with minimal losses, but the battle had not yet concluded and there was still a chance to snatch catastrophe from the jaws of triumph. ➤➤

The sweeping Balaklava Plain by Roger Fenton, 1855.

Galloping into Infamy

As the Russian infantry began their retreat from the three redoubts they still held, they dragged the abandoned British artillery with them. Raglan paled at the thought of losing guns to the enemy and issued an instruction as vague as so many of his others.

"Lord Raglan wishes the cavalry to advance rapidly to the front — follow the enemy and try to prevent the enemy carrying away the guns," it read. As the messenger, Captain Louis Nolan of the 15th (The King's) Regiment of (Light) Dragoons (Hussars), pulled away, Raglan shouted after him: "Tell Lord Lucan the cavalry is to attack immediately."

From where they were situated, Lucan was not sure what guns Raglan was alluding to. He knew the redoubts were in Russian hands and there were British guns there, but he also knew there were Russian guns on Fediukhin Heights which covered the Russian cavalry's retreat, as well as Russian guns installed at the eastern edge of the North Valley. Asking Nolan for clarity yielded only an impatient gesture towards the Causeway Heights and North Valley beyond: "There, my lord, is the enemy, there are your guns."

The Light Brigade risked spending another engagement doing nothing. The men were desperate to soak their sabres in blood. Unlike the Heavy Brigade, which consisted of armoured dragoons on heavy chargers and served as the army shock troop, the Light Brigade were unarmoured lancers and hussars whose role was skirmishing and reconnaissance. They were ill-served for a frontal assault, especially into the blazing barrels of enemy artillery at the end of the North Valley, galloping through the crossfire from Fediukhin Heights to the left and the Russians on Causeway Heights to their right. The loss was to become one of the most

"The Light Brigade risked spending another engagement doing nothing."

BELOW: A view of Balaklava harbour from the camp of the 93rd (Sutherland Highlanders) Regiment of Foot.

'The Thin Red Line', painted by Robert Gibb 25 years after the events it depicts, but no less stirring as a result.

BATTLE OF BALAKLAVA, 25TH OCTOBER, 1854.
The indicated positions of the troops show approximately how they were placed when orders to attack were given by the British Brigadiers

notorious in British military history: 661 men rode out, 113 were killed, 134 wounded and 45 taken prisoner - 292 men were lost in total, and with them some 362 horses. To their credit, these bold hussars got in amongst the Russian guns and drove them from the field - and the Russians had failed to achieve their objectives - but the needless slaughter was difficult for the British public to stomach. Reports in the press would contrast the nobility and gallantry of the cavalry with the self-serving incompetence of their commanders.

In a matter of minutes, a pallor had been cast over the defiant heroism of the Battle of Balaklava. The Russians had fallen short of their objective, but their continued presence at the end of the North Valley denied the British the use of the road along Causeway Heights, they claimed a bloody bill and had the guns to show for it. The cannon were paraded through

ABOVE: This map shows the two main phases of the battle co-currently, the Russian charge on the 93rd and the Heavy Brigade's intervention in the South Valley, and the starting position of the Light Brigade in the North Valley.

The 93rd (Sutherland Highlanders) Regiment of Foot resting on manoeuvres in Britain in 1860, by the prolific military artist Orlando Norie.

Sevastopol and soldiers showed off their trophies - tunics, shakos, and sabres - to the cheering crowds. It was a British victory, but one that left a bitter taste in the mouth of the victors.

The Tangled Legacy

The Battle of Balaklava would see the forging of two potent military myths that sculpted a new self-image for Britain's fighting men. The most commanding and influential of the two is, of course, the 'Charge of the Light Brigade' - immortalised in verse by Lord Alfred Tennyson - by which cavalry flung themselves into certain death as a matter of duty and dash. For the infantry, Balaklava was the exchange in which the concept of the 'The Thin Red Line' was honed. This phrase conjures up the dogged determination of the British soldier to hold firm no matter what happens against impossible odds. ➤➤

The Battle of Balaklava was followed by another attack on the British positions at the Battle of Inkerman (November 5, 1854), the cost of which was almost too much to bear. Further tested by the harsh winter, Great Britain entered 1855 a junior partner in the alliance with France and it was the French Army which took on responsibility for the increasingly brittle right flank of the allied position and ultimately cracked open Sevastopol at the Battle of Malakoff (September 8, 1855).

The Crimean War was costly in the extreme, and remembered primarily for its blunders, negligence and the spent lives, but it did successfully put paid to Russian designs on swallowing up the Black Sea and threatening British and French dominance of the Mediterranean. Arguably the greatest impact it had on the British Empire, however, was in signalling the need for urgent reform of the British Army and the beginning of a working

ABOVE: 'The Relief of the Light Brigade' by the late Victorian military artist Richard Caton Woodville, 1897, shows the 11th Hussars and 17th Lancers among the Russian guns.

relationship with the French - once Great Britain's most implacable foes - that would prove vital in the challenges of the late 19th century and early 20th.

Despite having fought so bitterly in the defence of Ottoman integrity, both Britain and France spent the last two decades of the 19th century increasing their grip on the sultan's territories in North Africa, the French taking Tunisia in 1881 and the British occupying Egypt in 1882.

LEFT: 'Valley of the Shadow of Death' by Roger Fenton, 1855. The view down the North Valley from the west shows the ground littered with cannon balls.

BELOW: The armoured dragoons of the Heavy Brigade charge at the Russian cavalry at 100 yards, taking them by surprise.

"Great Britain entered 1855 a junior partner in the alliance with France..."

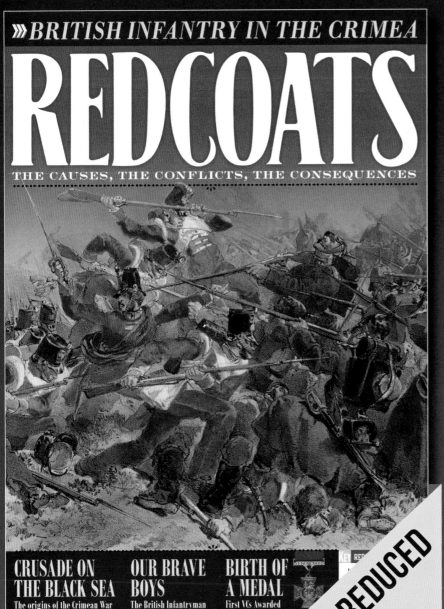

Mutiny on the Gomti

The Siege of Lucknow, May 30 - November 27, 1857

In deference to the fiction of the last Mughal Emperor - his writ going no further than his own palace - there was no British garrison stationed in the walled city of Delhi. As the sepoys rose and fell upon the once imperial capital, nine officers from the Ordnance Corps led by Lieutenant George Willoughby fought for five hours to prevent the palace armoury falling into rebel hands, eventually blowing the magazine to deny it to the enemy. Only three of the nine made it out alive and all three were awarded the Victoria Cross.

As the northern provinces of India simmered with insurrection, reinforcements were slow to arrive. Loyal troops were scattered over a vast distance and with only fledgling infrastructure, news travelled slowly and imperfectly. In short, the East India Company administration was slow to recognise the scale of the threat.

As swiftly as they could, the East India Company assembled a 3,000-strong Delhi Field Force in order to retake the vital city, drawing available troops from across the region - including the ill-starred garrison at Lucknow. The Siege of Delhi (June 8 – September 21, 1857) lasted four months with the vastly outnumbered Field Force digging in on a ridge overlooking the city to face a siege themselves. Eventually, with a daring final offensive, the city was retaken at a total cost of 1,254 British killed, 4,493 wounded, and another 29 Victoria Crosses awarded.

All of this, of course, meant that Lucknow was more or less alone. ➤➤

BELOW: 93rd Highlanders rush the bricked up doorway to Secundra Bagh which had been re-opened by British artillery. Watercolour by Orlando Norie, 1857.

The Battle in Context

ABOVE: An unsigned 1857 watercolour of rebels being blasted by British guns, a Mughal-era punishment called the 'Devil's Wind'.

By 1857, the Honourable East India Company all but ruled the subcontinent as an immense corporate fiefdom with only nominal oversight - principally in matters of politics - from the governor-general, the Crown's agent in India.

The current incumbent, James Broun-Ramsay, 1st Marquess of Dalhousie, had done much to build a modern state but just as much to awaken a widespread atmosphere of disquiet. Dalhousie firmly believed that all of India needed to be brought directly under British rule and to that end he introduced the Doctrine of Lapse which negated an indigenous ruler's traditional right to name their successor, meaning that if the ailing maharaja or nawab passed away without a son, his lands would instead be administered by the British. Dalhousie's more high-minded reforms, mainly concerning the welfare of women - providing for their education, allowing Hindu widows to remarry - further alienated traditionalists, who began to see an attack on their culture in every missionary or school, railway line or telegraph wire.

One of the few spheres where Indians were organised in great numbers, these tensions bubbled over in the Bengal Army where the sepoys already felt disaffected by new terms of service which forced them to serve outside of Bengal in peacetime (without the compensation earned whilst doing so in times of conflict) and a new requirement to serve overseas was anathema to observant Hindus. According to the text of the *Dharmasūtra*, kala pani ('black water' in Sanskrit) - the act of crossing an ocean - led to spiritual pollution and the breaking of the cycle of reincarnation. The rapid expansion of the colonial infrastructure had also created a drain on educated and efficient European officers, leaving the sepoys to be ministered by the unremarkable, incompetent, criminal, and disinterested.

Against this backdrop, the new Enfield Pattern 1853 rifle-musket was issued. The rifling (spiral) in the barrel allowed the musket ball to be fired further and with greater accuracy, but to load it the soldier bit the head off a greased paper cartridge containing black powder and a musket ball. Rumours began to circulate that the grease was made from the mixed fat of both pigs and cows, the former haram (prohibited) to Muslims and the latter sacred to Hindus.

The company responded with a disastrous lack of sensitivity. In April 1857 in Meerut, a garrison town 40 miles east of Delhi, a group of 85 sepoys who refused to use their new rifles were court martialled, clapped in irons and given long prison sentences. Their comrades broke them out, killed their officers, and then marched on Delhi where they joined with the local garrison with the intention of restoring the authority of the decaying Mughal Emperor, Bahadur Shah II - a royal relic on a company pension. Risings were mainly concentrated in the north, around the Bengal Army and the newly-annexed Princely State of Oudh (now Uttar Pradesh), whose king had been vilified and tossed into exile so that Dalhousie could claim it under the Doctrine of Lapse. Oudh supplied three-fourths of all rebels in the Indian Mutiny and two-thirds of all recruits to the 120,000-strong Bengal Army.

The bloodlust of the rebels - who killed any Christians and Europeans they were able to find in Delhi and in Cawnpore massacred around 900 men, women and children who had been promised safe passage - was answered by the British. Most infamously, they resurrected the old Mughal punishment of binding rebels to the mouths of cannons and then firing it, the disintegration of the poor soul's body was called the 'devil's wind'.

RIGHT: Sepoys murdering British soldiers and civilians at Cawnpore, by R. M. Jephson circa 1900. Note the baby on the bayonet.

ABOVE: An 1826 painting by an unknown Indian artist of Lucknow viewed from the River Gomti. As the historic capital of the Princely State of Oudh, it was home to many beautiful palaces, temples and mosques.

Playing for Time

As the province at the heart of the Indian Mutiny and the site of a heavy-handed recent annexation, it was inevitable that the rebels would march on Oudh's royal capital. Although Brigadier General Sir Henry Lawrence, chief commissioner of Oudh, believed his sepoys would remain loyal, he directed Europeans to take shelter in Lucknow's British Residency, a scenic 60-acre estate protected by four entrenched artillery batteries. He also began to stockpile supplies necessary for their survival and ordered public hangings of conspirators in groups of two. Despite his optimism, of the 4,000 or so Bengal Army sepoys stationed in and around Lucknow, only approximately 700 remained by his side throughout the siege.

An old colonial hand who spoke Urdu, Hindi and Persian, Lawrence had been instrumental in the successful integration of Punjab into the British Empire, placating the Sikh aristocracy with large pensions and the people by reducing taxes and the punitive rights of landlords, whilst outlawing traditional practises such as the suicide of widows on their husband's funeral pyres (called suttee, from the Sanskrit meaning 'good woman'), infanticide of girls, and the use of forced labour. He had been dispatched to Oudh to do from Lucknow what he had managed to do from Lahore, and his deft diplomatic hand managed to keep rebellion at bay and buy the defenders time.

Hearing that a group of 'several hundred' rebels were on the move, Lawrence - old and infirm, his fighting days well behind him - was convinced by his more gung-ho subordinates to

try and cut them off on the road. Taking three companies of 32nd Regiment of Foot, plus detachments from other regiments numbering approximately 700 men, he discovered that the approaching force was closer to 7,000-strong.

The Battle of Chinhat (June 30, 1857) was a rude awakening indeed. The rebels were well organised by Barkat Ahmad, a former risaldar (cavalry captain) in the company's Bengal Army. Immediately fired on by the larger force and flanked by the rebel cavalry, many of Lawrence's sepoys defected - the Bengal Native Artillery overturning their guns and joining the rebels - whilst his Sikh horsemen simply bolted. Only a series of valiant delaying actions bought the survivors time to limp back into Lucknow.

Roughly 1,720 troops were now tasked with the protection of 1,280 British civilians and an estimated 8,000 rebels soon took up positions

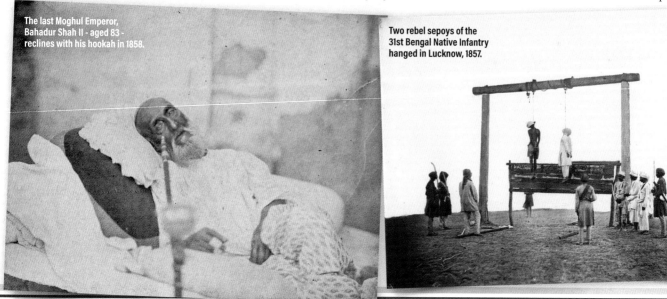

The last Moghul Emperor, Bahadur Shah II - aged 83 - reclines with his hookah in 1858.

Two rebel sepoys of the 31st Bengal Native Infantry hanged in Lucknow, 1857.

in the city. Though protected on one side by a low stone wall and an earthen redoubt on the other, the cluster of buildings which made up the Residency was easily within range of snipers and artillery spotters from the towers and minarets in the heart of Lucknow.

The diplomat's instincts had won out over those of the brigadier general. When Lawrence's engineers had recommended levelling nearby mosques, palaces and other historic structures, Lawrence refused out of concern that it would antagonise the townsfolk who until then had been peaceable. However,

The ruins of the British Residency, photographed in 1865 by Samuel Bourne.

ABOVE: A full-length portrait of Brigadier General Sir Henry Havelock, the 'Hero of Lucknow,' who died before the Residency could be evacuated. Hand-coloured engraving by Alexander Ritchie, 1859.

on July 4, Lawrence was killed by shrapnel when a shell struck his room and command passed to Colonel John Inglis, 32nd Foot.

Rather than waiting for his cot to be shelled next, Inglis pursued a policy of aggressive defence and kept the rebels at bay with a series of sorties and raids. Though the mutineers lacked a unified leadership, many of them were experienced officers and they put their siege craft to use against the men who had trained them. On August 5, a mine was spotted and successfully counter-mined by the British.

The First Relief Attempt

Meanwhile, Brigadier General Sir Henry Havelock had retaken Cawnpore but was he unable to press on until he had been reinforced. The intense heat of summer, fresh casualties, and attendant disease had sapped the strength of his force and only when he was joined by Major General Sir James Outram did, they have the numbers to march on Lucknow. Although Outram was senior, he conceded command to Havelock so that he might enjoy the glory of Lucknow's relief. Outram then volunteered his services as a cavalry commander. ➤➤

BELOW: An 1864 watercolour of the British Residency in Lucknow by William Simpson, showing the devastation following the siege.

On September 18, 1857, they marched north with a relief force of 2,500 men. In the wake of the heavy monsoon rains, Havelock found himself unable to flank the city and was forced to keep to the road and fight through the narrow streets of Lucknow. The cost was so great as they crossed the Charbagh Canal that Outram argued in favour of spending the night in the Fort of Machchi Bhawan, which was less than two miles northwest of their destination. Havelock argued for pushing on through the darkness, terrified that the Residency would be overwhelmed and slaughtered if they dragged their heels.

Although successful in fighting his way through to the Residency, Havelock brought little relief to the garrison. The hard-fighting frontal assault had cost the relief force 535 casualties and the would-be rescuers had no choice but to join the besieged behind the pock-marked walls of the Residency.

Conditions for the besieged were grim. The heaps of dead men and animals in Lucknow attracted a Biblical volume of flies, rats, and malevolent black carrion birds. The burial of the dead became a constant duty for those not engaged in the compound's defence. Food was beginning to run out, disease reduced the number of effective defenders by over half and the rebels continued to mine the defences. In retaliation, the defenders dug 21 vertical shafts and 3,291 feet of horizontal tunnel to collapse the enemy tunnels and earthworks.

Only by accident did Outram - who assumed command once Havelock had achieved his objective - discover that the late Brig Gen Lawrence had hidden a significant quantity of supplies beneath the Residency but had been killed before he could inform anyone. This restored their spirits and the will to fight. Under Outram's leadership, the defenders increased their perimeter as far as the palaces

ABOVE: A bayonet charge of British infantry against rebel sepoys by E. S. Hardy, 1900. Note the soldiers wearing white covered forage caps as protection against the sun.

of Farhat Baksh and Chattar Manzil southeast along the River Gomti, although the number of rebels descending on the city continued to grow and the rebel artillery hammered the Residency from the northern banks of the Gomti.

The Second Relief Attempt

A second relief force of 4,500 under the newly-arrived Lt Gen Sir Colin Campbell - a hero of the Battle of Balaklava sent to assume command of the loyal Bengal Army - arrived on November 16, 1857. By now the number of rebels in and around Lucknow was estimated to be well over 30,000, but lines of communication had been established between Cawnpore and the Residency. Unlike his predecessors, Campbell was not fighting blind.

ABOVE: The inner courtyard of Secundra Bagh in 1858, the ground littered with bones which had been disinterred by the photographer to add dramatic impact to the image.

He advanced from the east, crossing the empty canal which had been drained by the rebels to flood the river, and then stormed the Secundra Bagh - an ornate summer residence amid a walled garden - under intense fire from the mutineers who had transformed it into a bristling strong point.

The 93rd Highlanders and some men of the 4th Infantry, Punjab Irregular Force rushed a small bricked-up doorway which had been blasted open, whilst the rest of the 4th Punjabis attacked the main gateway. As they approached the rebels began to shut it and Subadar (captain) Mukarab Khan wedged his arm into the rapidly shrinking gap, doing untold damage but preventing the enemy from barring the gate to the British. Eighteen Victoria Crosses were recommended for that one encounter, although perhaps many more were deserved. Indians weren't eligible for the VC until 1914, although plenty of their white officers were and men like Mukarab Khan were forced to settle for the Indian Order of Merit.

ABOVE: A coloured lithograph from 1859 showing Brig Gen Havelock and Maj Gen Outram greeting Lt Gen Campbell.

With memories of the Cawnpore Massacre boiling their blood, the British set about bayonetting and shooting every mutineer they could find in the villa's courtyard, killing an estimated 2,500 men before moving on to open up a path to the British lines a mile-and-a-half to their west. The 4th Punjabis remained billeted in the wreckage of Secundra Bagh until the relief force was ready to withdraw.

On November 17, Campbell arrived at the Residency, by November 23 all of the haven's beleaguered occupants had been evacuated, and Campbell prepared to depart, leaving 4,000 men under Outram at nearby Alambagh to harry the rebels if they attempted operations outside of the city. His business concluded, on November 24, Lt Gen Havelock died following a sudden attack of dysentery. News of his death took so long to reach London compared to the jubilant tidings of the relief, that he was posthumously promoted to major general, given the colonelcy of the 3rd (East Kent) Regiment of Foot (The Buffs), and appointed a baronet.

It would be another four months before the rebellion in Lucknow was finally put down with Campbell retaking the city in a methodical building-by-building offensive over March 1 -14, 1858, with the largest army ever assembled in India.

The Rise of the Raj

Whilst Delhi was really the strategic heart of the rebellion and Cawnpore the site of some of its atrocities, it was the Siege of Lucknow that captured the public imagination. It went on to become the setting for numerous popular plays, novels, and patriotic poems, the most celebrated being, of course, Alfred Tennyson's *The Defence of Lucknow*.

In one respect the Indian Mutiny was successful. It was the end of East India Company rule. Instead of an inconsistent private enterprise which undertook nation-building as a side-project, India was placed under the direct control of Great Britain through its viceroy, who represented the Crown. This began a period known as the British Raj (Sanskrit for 'rule') and with it a series of wide-reaching reforms of military and civilian institutions. For the first time, Indians were consulted on their own governance by means of the Indian Councils Act of 1861, although the Legislative Council that it represented was a largely advisory body. A single legal code was introduced in 1860 and the following year a single national police service to enforce it.

Although many of Lord Dalhousie's cultural initiatives (including the Doctrine of Lapse) were rolled back, the failure of the continent's traditional leaders - the 'native princes' - to contribute any actual leadership during the Indian Mutiny was a far more effective blow to the traditionalists than sending women to school. Even the Mughal Emperor, Bahadur Shah II, a man who had lost so much through British rule was only ever a reluctant figurehead for the Indian Mutiny. He was forced into exile in Burma (now Myanmar) and died a few years later in 1862 at the grand old age of 87.

The technological innovations Dalhousie rolled out continued apace, however. Railways and telegraph lines soon crisscrossed the landscape, along with factories, irrigation ditches, and roads. As it had done in Britain a century earlier, this industrial revolution led to the rapid growth of an educated and urban middle class, and it and it would be they who carried the torch of Indian nationalism through the remaining 89 years of colonial control and all the way to independence.

"Banner of England, not for a season, O banner of Britain, hast thou
Floated in conquering battle or flapt to the battle-cry!
Never with mightier glory than when we had rear'd thee on high
Flying at top of the roofs in the ghastly siege of Lucknow—
Shot thro' the staff or the halyard, but ever we raised thee anew,
And ever upon the topmost roof our banner of England blew."
'The Defence of Lucknow', Alfred Tennyson (1879)

The long train of evacuees from Lucknow makes its way into Cawnpore on November 28, 1857. Lithograph from 1859.

On January 17, 1879, Lieutenant John Chard, Royal Engineers arrived at Rorke's Drift. Placed in charge of the pontoon bridge across the Buffalo River, he immediately set to work with his team of sappers to patch up this vital artery of the British advance into Zululand. By no stretch of the imagination was Rorke's Drift the frontline of the Anglo-Zulu War, it was simply a crossing point for the army of Major General Frederic Thesiger, 2nd Baron Chelmsford, much as it had been the crossing point for traders and missionaries for decades.

Rorke's Drift had been settled as a farm in 1849 by an Irishman called James Rorke, who built himself a single-storey farmhouse with a thatched roof and 11 rooms, five of which could only be accessed from the outside, so they could be rented to lodgers. Rorke also built a small store of the same simple brick and thatch design. Both buildings had wide verandas.

When Rorke died his property was acquired by the Norwegian Missionary Society with a view to using it as a base from which to take the word of God to Zululand. Reverend Otto Witt took up residence and turned the store into a chapel. He also renamed the hill behind the station Oscarberg. The wooden cattle kraal, meaning enclosure, northeast of the chapel was replaced by a more robust stonewalled one. There was also a smaller stone kraal directly adjoining the chapel.

Army doctrine maintained that an engineer working in the field must be accompanied by infantry, as he hadn't been left any and the pontoon was too far from the mission to be covered by its guns, Chard headed up towards the new camp at Isandlwana for clarification. He was told that Chelmsford and his staff had already set off on a Zulu hunt, although Chard's fears had been accounted for and a battalion of reinforcements were expected from Helpmekaar in Natal. As he turned back towards Rorke's Drift, Chard noted with some foreboding that Zulu warriors were already visible on the hills. The Battle of Isandlwana would begin within hours and tens of thousands of Zulu would sweep into the camp, slaughtering over 1,300 of the 1,837 men left holding Chelmsford's supplies. ➤➤

Zulu Storm

The Defence of Rorke's Drift, January 22-23, 1879

BELOW: 'The Defence of Rorke's Drift' by Alphonse de Neuville. This famous painting includes a number of individuals involved in the battle, from left to right: Assistant Commissary Walter Dunne (in blue, moving a biscuit box), Private Henry Hook (in blue, carrying a man on his back) Private Frederick Hitch (with his head bandaged, behind Bromhead), Lieutenant Gonville Bromhead (standing in the middle of the compound pointing), Surgeon-Major James Reynolds (attending to Dalton's wound with his terrier), Acting Assistant Commissary James Dalton (sitting in the foreground with a shoulder wound), Chaplain George Smith (the bearded man with his hand in his ammunition sack), Corporal Ferdinand Schiess (in the tan uniform, stabbing a Zulu with his bayonet), and Lieutenant John Chard (bare headed with the grey breeches and rifle)

was a clear obstacle to a single South Africa. A series of incredibly thin casus belli were contrived in order for the British high commissioner to South Africa, Sir Henry Bartle Frere, to level an ultimatum that would effectively turn Zululand into a British protectorate.

Although he could mobilise perhaps as many as 60,000 warriors, each one with a religious imperative to disembowel their foe after he had been slain, Cetshwayo pleaded with the British for peace. However, the ultimatum was not designed to be met, it was designed to be answered with war.

In January 1879, three columns of British troops entered Zululand at various points with the intention of converging on the capital, Ulundi. The largest of them under the command of Major General Frederic Thesiger, 2nd Baron Chelmsford crossed the Buffalo River at Rorke's Drift before setting up camp at Isandlwana. They neglected to circle their wagons into a protective formation that the Boers called a 'laager' and Chelmsford took most of the force into the hills to chase down a phantom Zulu army. Having lured most of the defenders away from their supplies, the Zulu descended in strength on the camp making a massacre of the remaining force at the Battle of Isandlwana (January 22, 1879), and leaving the skeleton force at Rorke's Drift to face the oncoming storm.

LEFT: Cetshwayo kaMpande, the last independent king of the Zulu, pictured in 1878.

BELOW: The Zulu charge at the British line at Isandlwana. Spread too thinly to cover almost a mile of front, not even volley fire could halt the onslaught.

Southern Africa was not yet South Africa, nor did the Anglo-Zulu War bring it into being, but towards the end of the 19th century Britain's architects of empire began to dream of uniting their colonies into a single self-governing (and self-funding) state. They ignored not just the disparity between the wealthy Cape Colony, which had begun as a Dutch settlement in 1652, and the less developed and more recently established Natal Colony, but also the fact that two of the white colonies Britain counted in its orbit weren't even run by Britain. The Orange Free State and the South African Republic (also known as the Transvaal Republic) were independent republics, dominated by Boers, deeply religious settlers of mostly Dutch descent who had moved deeper and deeper inland to escape the meddling of the British.

Despite the white dominance of southern Africa which had seen successive black states pushed back, beaten down and then absorbed outright, Zululand to the immediate north of Natal and east of Transvaal remained a belligerent exception. It had expanded rapidly during the 18th century to become the most powerful indigenous nation below the Sahara thanks to the innovative tactics and weapons of its first king, Shaka Zulu. Under Shaka, Zululand had become a warrior state in which its men were groomed from birth to live and fight in regiments and even under Shaka's less impressive successors, the Zulu Kingdom was a source of intense anxiety for Boer and Briton alike.

Despite their reputation for ferocity, by 1879 the Zulu king, Cetshwayo kaMpande, counted himself as an ally of the British, who had backed him in border disputes with Transvaal and had been welcoming to both missionaries and merchants. The short-lived annexation of Transvaal in 1877 proved, however, that the British were fairweather friends to their black neighbours.

The subjugation of the Zulu now promised three benefits: reversing the earlier border claims might endear them to the Boers who were beginning to chaff under British rule, Zulu would flood the labour market, driving costs down and feeding the hungry diamond fields, and an independent black state

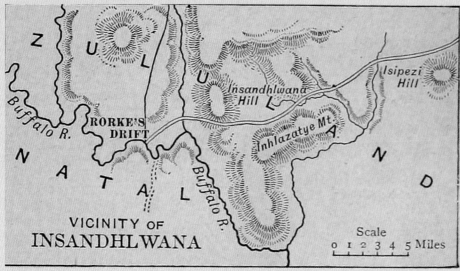

ABOVE: A map showing the site of the battle in relation to Isandlwana and Isipezi, where Lord Chelmsford's force was heading on January 22, 1879.

The Unlikely Heroes

Despite his depiction in the 1964 film, *Zulu*, Otto Witt was not a gimlet-eyed hysteric cursing the British Army and predicting doom (though he did later sue them successfully for destruction of property). On the outbreak of the Anglo-Zulu War, he made the mission available to the British and was paid a rent for his trouble. Witt moved his family away from the border in January 1879 and joined them himself just prior to the attack.

The army's Commissariat and Transport Corps had transformed the chapel back into a storeroom, filled with bags of mealie (local grain), ammunition, and other supplies required for Chelmsford's column. The house, meanwhile, had been taken over by the Army Medical Department and was occupied by the column's 35 miscellaneous wounded.

Assistant Commissary Walter Dunne was in charge of the stores, while the field hospital was the domain of Surgeon Major James Henry Reynolds, his three staff and his terrier, Dick. Dunne was joined by the impressive and soon to be heroic figure of Acting Assistant Commissary James Langley Dalton.

One of the men most ill-served by *Zulu*, rather than a genteel battle-shy administrator, Dalton had been in uniform since the age of 17 and worked his way up through the ranks to corporal and then staff sergeant. He had been discharged in 1871 and emigrated to Africa when the war brought a new opportunity to serve. Though technically a civilian, the 44-year-old was the most experienced man stationed at the mission.

Major Henry Spalding, 104th Regiment of Foot, was the commanding officer of Rorke's Drift. A member of Chelmsford's staff in charge of communication and supplies, Spalding had served in the Indian Mutiny but otherwise remained a fairly anonymous soldier. The striking figure of Chaplain George Smith was also present. Smith had been working as a missionary in Africa since 1870.

Protecting Rorke's Drift were B Company, 1/24th Regiment of Foot under Lieutenant Gonville Bromhead. Unlike the sharp and sneering Michael Caine of the film, 'Gonny' was popular with the men but seen as useless by his peers. Partially deaf and regarded as being lazy, his weaknesses in the field were concealed by the regiment who made sure that he was always left in positions where he would not be putting lives at risk. With Rorke's Drift safely behind the lines and B Company's commander Captain Alfred

> *"Unlike the sharp and sneering Michael Caine of the film, 'Gonny' was popular with the men but seen as useless by his peers."*

BELOW: Tiny against Oscarberg and the distant Buffalo River, Rorke's Drift is dwarfed by the landscape in this photograph.

ABOVE: How the mission station appeared prior to the outbreak of the Anglo-Zulu War, with the chapel to the left and the house on the right, and Oscarberg looming behind.

The traditional Zulu attack formation was the 'horns of the buffalo' in which the warriors in the centre pinned the enemy in place whilst the two 'horns' dug into their flanks. During the Battle of Isandlwana, part of the right horn of the Zulu attack had overshot the camp in too broad a sweep and returned to the field to discover that the battle had already won. Their blood was up, and they felt cheated out of victory. Three regiments of as many as 4,000 warriors under the command of Dabulamanzi kaMpande, the Zulu king Cetshwayo kaMpande's half-brother, were heading for the mission station.

Independently of one another, the news had reached Chard and Bromhead already. Two colonial officers had appeared from the direction of Isandlwana and raced towards the Chard at the crossing to relay that Isandlwana had fallen, only a handful had managed to escape, and behind them a Zulu war party was bearing down on Rorke's Drift.

Back at the camp, Bromhead received a message from Cap Edward Essex, one of the only staff officers to survive Isandlwana, with orders. They were to strengthen the defences and hold the mission at all costs. Bromhead dispatched a rider to the garrison at Helpmekaar with an update while Dalton, who had experience of constructing field works, ordered the collapsing of the tents to offer a clear field of fire, linking the two buildings with a perimeter of biscuit boxes and mealie bags, and bashing firing holes into the walls of the hospital with pickaxes.

Chard and Bromhead quickly compared notes. Chard's prognosis was gloomy. He wanted the two wagons loaded and the garrison to vacate, but the sober Dalton proved the voice of reason: if they left on foot, they would be overtaken by the ➤➤

Godwin Austen having been accidentally shot by one of his own men, looking after the supply depot was the most suitable appointment.

Bromhead's rock was Colour Sergeant Frank Bourne, who on the screen is depicted as the archetypal statuesque NCO. In actuality, Bourne was 5' 5" tall, 23-years-old, and softly spoken, but he could read and write, and had such an affinity for army life that he scaled the ranks rapidly. The youngest NCO in the British Army, he was nicknamed 'The Kid'. Also on hand were 100 poorly trained black auxiliaries of 2/3rd Natal Native Contingent under Cap William Stephenson, a colonial officer who spoke the local languages.

Man the Barricades

Chard returned to Rorke's Drift and explained the situation at Isandlwana to Spalding. With only 200 defenders, and only half of them British regulars with the new breech-loading Martini-Henry rifles, Rorke's Drift suddenly felt incredibly exposed. In his wisdom, Spalding decided to head 10 miles up the road to Helpmekaar to hurry the promised reinforcements along. Just before he left, he paused and asked Chard who was the senior of, himself or Bromhead. Stephenson was an irregular, and as a surgeon, Reynolds could not command line infantry.

Spalding's copy of the *Army List* revealed that Chard had been commissioned a lieutenant in 1868 and Bromhead in 1871.

Under the old system Bromhead purchased his commission of ensign in 1867, a junior rank that was phased out in 1871 resulting in an automatic promotion to lieutenant which was not exactly a glowing endorsement.

At around 3.15pm, Witt, Reynolds, and Smith - the missionary, the surgeon, and the chaplain - were keeping watch from Oscarberg when they heard distant rifle fire and spotted Zulus crossing the Buffalo River into Natal. They rushed back to warn the camp.

ABOVE: Taken at his brother Cetshwayo kaMpande's coronation in 1873, the impulsive Dabulamanzi kaMpande stands at the centre of this photograph. He would go on to command the Zulu at the Battle of Rorke's Drift. Wellcome Collection CC BY 4.0

ABOVE: John Chard pictured later in his career in the uniform of a major of the Royal Engineers. He is wearing his Victoria Cross.

BELOW: Zulu warriors fling themselves at the barricade. At points, the piles of dead were so deep that the Zulu could scramble up them to clear the mealie bags.

Zulu and slaughtered on open ground. In contrast to the film which presents Chard as heroic from the outset, it was the acting assistant commissary who strengthened the lieutenant's resolve to fight.

The Last Betrayal

The flow of stragglers was punctuated by the stirring sight of an 80-man column of the elite Natal Native Horse led by Lieutenant Alfred Henderson who placed his troop at Chard's disposal. They had broken through the Zulu cordon and charged straight down the road to Rorke's Drift, where they joined the defenders. Henderson's men rode out around the drift and the south face of Oscarberg with orders to delay the Zulu advance for as long as possible.

The pontoon briefly caused Chard some concern - it was after all his reason for being there. He decided to stake the pontoons in the centre of the Buffalo River, where hopefully they would be left alone by the fighting. The two men responsible for manning the crossing offered to stay and fight off any Zulu who tried to interfere. It was a near suicidal commitment to duty even by the standards of the Victorian army and Chard dismissed it.

Linking the hospital to the store left the defenders severely overstretched, but some of the patients could not be moved from their cots. As the doors opened outwards from the hastily erected compound, Bromhead picked six men to defend the three exposed rooms - locking themselves in with ample ammunition to defend the patients. Those patients mobile or cognizant enough to wield a rifle were to join the fight.

At 4.30pm B Company, those of the Natal Native Contingent with rifles, and a handful of the hospital's walking wounded were manning the perimeter with bayonets fixed. The men of the NNC armed with throwing spears and cowhide shields sheltered in the stone cattle kraal. In front of the store, a pyramid of unused mealie sacks towered over the defenders and Dalton had ordered a dozen boxes of ammunition opened so that the men could stuff their pouches with rounds.

Gunfire was heard around the south face of Oscarberg and at 4.30pm the Natal Native Horse raced past in full retreat, one of them shouting out in his native language that they were doomed. The black auxiliaries panicked and bolted in their wake, and to the disgust of the defenders Stephenson joined them. As an

"Under the fierce defence and covering fire from the hospital, the first wave melted away and disappeared..."

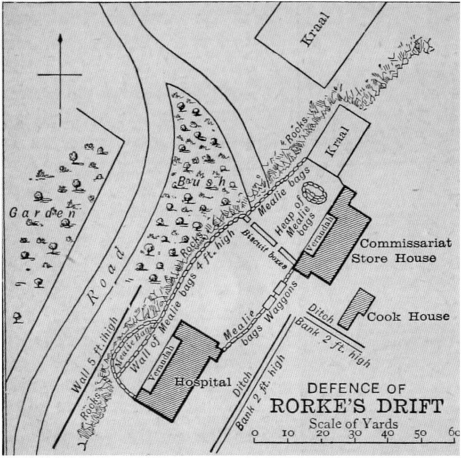

ABOVE: An illustration of the mission and its defences.

back behind an inner wall of biscuit boxes between the store and the hospital that reduced the perimeter by two thirds. It was either that or risk the mission being entirely overrun, but Chard's decision left six soldiers and 24 wounded stranded in the hospital building.

Now surrounding the hospital on three sides, the Zulu flung flaming spear after flaming spear onto the sodden thatch until it caught light. The only external door which had not been barricaded ahead of the battle opened onto the veranda which was now firmly in Zulu hands.

In the southeast corner room was a single NNC warrior with broken legs and Privates Henry Hook and Robert Cole, who fired through their loopholes into the attacking Zulu. Unlike the unscrupulous rogue of *Zulu* - created presumably for the sake of having a redemptive character arc - the real Hook was an upstanding soldier, Methodist and teetotaller. He was not in the hospital as a malingerer, but as the cook. Cole left early on, but Hook held firm.

The outer door was covered by a mattress and a stack of mealie sacks, and as smoke began to fill the room Hook broke through the inner door and left the immobile African levy to his death. He was confronted by nine more patients and unwilling to leave them to their fate, he sealed up the door he had come through just as the Zulu burst into the room behind him.

In another room Ptes John and Joseph Williams had been defending four patients. No relation, B Company had several men named Jones and Williams, but its 'Welsh' character has been severely overstated. Although the 24th had moved to Brecon in 1873, many of the men had been ➤➤

irregular, he was unable to face court martial but his career as a colonial officer was over. Including the wounded and non-combatants, there were now 139 men left to hold Rorke's Drift against the oncoming foe.

Beating Them Back
The first wave of Zulu crashed around Oscarberg and flung themselves at the southern wall of the field hospital and store. The defenders opened fire wildly at 500 yards but with the narrowest face of the mission towards the enemy, the Zulu made it to within 60 yards before they were torn to shreds by the firing line.

A larger chunk of the attackers veered left around the hospital to the northwestern corner of the stockade where they pressed right up to the barricade itself through sheer force of numbers. Bromhead, wielding his revolver, and Dalton with a rifle led the fierce hand-to-hand resistance. The pressure was such that the defenders were forced back towards the front of the hospital, their bayonets held steadily forward.

Under the fierce defence and covering fire from the hospital, the first wave melted away and disappeared behind the wall of the garden to the northwest of the mission. By now hundreds of Zulu were scattered on the southern face of Oscarberg, firing

down on Rorke's Drift from behind rocks and caves with the rifles they had taken from Isandlwana. The men sheltering in the garden, and another group of Zulus in the stone kraal to the northeast also peppered the barricades with gunfire.

As the light began to fade, the Zulus kept up their assault on the hospital and the northwest wall. Corporal Christian Schiess, a Swiss-born NCO in the Natal Native Contingent and not an officer of the Natal Mounted Police as the film claims, had limped from the hospital to join the defenders on the barricade. A powerfully built veteran of the Franco-Prussian War (1870-1871), he proved himself a demon with the bayonet.

Chaplain Smith made the rounds too. He was unable to bear arms as a man of faith, but he worked his way around the line distributing ammunition and asking the men not to swear so much, which earned him respect, mirth and the nickname 'Ammunition Smith.'

The Hospital Aflame
At 6pm, Dabulamanzi ordered the last major push of the day: a simultaneous offensive on both the south and north walls. It was the sort of co-ordinated action that the defenders had been dreading, and Chard ordered the men

ABOVE: Chard and Bromhead direct the defence while the men wait for the Zulu attack with bayonets fixed.

ABOVE: The frantic close quarter fighting at the barricade saw men use their rifles as clubs.

of his Martini-Henry. Hook wrenched it from his grasp and shot the Zulu dead.

Hook and Williams pushed through into the next room and then the room beyond, in which Ptes Robert and William Jones were protecting six patients. While the two Joneses covered the door with their bayonets, Hook and Williams lowered the patients six feet from a high northeast-facing window to the ground where they could make a dash across 40-yard killing field for the inner wall of biscuit boxes. With the defenders offering covering fire, most of them made it.

One man had been missed - Pte Waters had hidden in a cupboard and Hook had moved right past him - and another could not be moved. The Joneses had fought valiantly to protect their charges. Robert had been stabbed three times and was growing weak with blood loss, only the spread of fire saved him - throwing its orange curtain between the Zulu and the soldiers so that William could help Robert through the window.

Tooth and Nail

Though buoyed by the sight of the burning field hospital, the Zulu were traditionally wary of fighting at night. From a purely practical standpoint command and control was impossible when the commander could not see what his warriors were doing, but there were supernatural threats too. In the darkness malign forces called umnyama cast their baleful presence on the deeds of men.

recruited from the industrial Midlands. There would be no throaty renditions of 'Men of Harlech'.

Theirs was one of the rooms with no internal door and when their ammunition ran out, Joseph Jones and two of the patients had been dragged from the room by the Zulu while the others hacked at the internal wall of crude mud and brick with their bayonets. From there, Jones dug his way into Hook's new location.

Hook and Williams now had 11 patients, a shoddily reinforced door through which the Zulu could break in and only one possible route of escape: making another hole in another wall. While Hook covered the door with his bayonet, Williams took a pickaxe to the far wall. By now the internal door was open and one at a time, the Zulu were trying to force their way in. An assegai glanced off the regimental crest on Hook's sun helmet and a warrior leapt forward to grab the barrel

"Though bouyed by the sight of the burning hospital, the Zulu were traditionally wary of fighting at night."

BELOW: Less well known than Neuville's painting, 'The Defense of Rorke's Drift' by Elizabeth Thompson, Lady Butler similarly shows the battle's significant individuals. In the middle Lieutenant Bromhead holds a sword while Lieutenant Chard points.

The concentrated offensives of the afternoon became a series of probing attacks. The hospital burned for hours, its glow aiding the British in picking their targets. On the far side of the mission from the hospital, the Zulu managed to drive the defenders from the small stone kraal abutting the northeast barricade.

Acting Assistant Commissary Dalton was leading the defence of a seven yard gap in the biscuit box wall until he was shot in the shoulder. Cpl Schiess distinguished himself too. Walking wounded already, Schiess vaulted the wall to bayonet a Zulu who had shot his helmet off, two more warriors ran at him and he shot one and stabbed the other. Later hit by a bullet that incredibly bounced off the back of his head and lodged in his shoulder, he continued to fight. Pte Hitch was shot too - a slug from a muzzle-loaded musket shattered his shoulder bone. Finding that his right arm would no longer move he tucked it into his belt and traded his rifle for Lt Bromhead's revolver so that he could continue to fight. Four hours later, Hitch passed out from blood loss and Reynolds picked out 36 shards of bone before sewing him back up.

Even within this reduced fortification and greater concentration of fire, the Zulu were poised to overrun Rorke's Drift and Assistant Commissary Dunne set about arranging the stack of unused mealie bags into a final circular redoubt for the defenders - the result stood 20 feet high and 12 feet wide.

The men fought on, deafened by the din of bullets, their throats hoarse and dry from the smoke and the shouting. Shoulders and biceps were bruised from the kick of the rifle a hundred times over, and many soldiers had swapped to their off hands to share the punishment with their opposite shoulders. Fingers were burnt from the overheated barrels - one or two could be seen glowing in

the dark - and some men had powder burns on their faces.

By now the Zulu appetite for battle was fading. They were getting spooked by reports that a British relief column was closing in on Rorke's Drift - indeed Maj Spalding was on his way back with two companies from Helpmekaar, gathering up refugees from Isandlwana en route and adding them to the force. As it happened, Spalding was to abandon Rorke's Drift twice. When they sighted the burning field hospital in the distance, the major decided that the mission had already fallen and turned his relief column back to Helpmekaar. Nonetheless, by 4.30am the Zulu guns had fallen silent.

Counting the Cost

As dawn broke over the smouldering mission, the defenders were stunned to see the Zulu army returning around the foot of Oscarberg, from where they had originally come. Seventeen defenders were dead, many more wounded - some seriously, but beyond the stockade lay heaps of Zulu dead. That they had spent 20,000 rounds of ammunition accounted for this staggering loss of life. Cautiously sending men out to gather the weapons they counted 351 Zulu fallen.

Hundreds more Zulu would die within days, lacking the medical knowledge to care for bullet wounds. The true death toll is impossible to count. At 8am a cheer went up as Chelmsford's column was spotted coming from the direction of Isandlwana. The men hugged each other in relief and a signal flag was waved from the roof of the storehouse. Within minutes mounted irregulars rode past

ABOVE: Major General Frederic Thesiger, pictured in 1870 while Adjutant General in India. Shortly after arriving in Africa he succeeded his father as Baron Chelmsford.

waving their hats and cheering and following them was Chelmsford.

Chard presented his report to the general, and then Chelmsford insisted on meeting some of the heroes of the night. He went on to make 11 recommendations for the Victoria Cross - the largest number ever awarded in a single action by one regiment - along with four Distinguished Conduct Medals. Chelmsford's mood had been lifted when he realised the scale of the miracle at Rorke's Drift. A heroic stand against all odds might be just the thing to rescue his reputation after the massacre of the previous day.

With the loss of so many men and stores, Chelmsford's formidable column was effectively out of action and the remaining columns were isolated, fighting defensively to maintain their now-precarious positions in Zululand. By May 1879, Chelmsford had been reinforced and he renewed his assault on the Zulu king, fighting methodically and cautiously to take Cetshwayo kaMpande's capital at the Battle of Ulundi (July 4, 1879). Now a failed state, Zululand became a protectorate of Cape Colony before disintegrating into civil war and being annexed outright by Natal. The most powerful black kingdom remaining in sub-Saharan Africa had been laid low and the British turned their attention to their stubbornly independently white neighbours, the Boers.

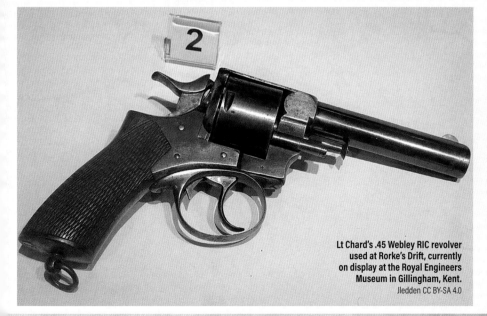

Lt Chard's .45 Webley RIC revolver used at Rorke's Drift, currently on display at the Royal Engineers Museum in Gillingham, Kent.
Jledden CC BY-SA 4.0

Ghosts of Gandamak

The Battle of Kandahar, September 1, 1880

Though Kabul, Jalalabad and the crucial mountain passes remained firmly under British control, to the west the ancient fortress of Kandahar suddenly seemed incredibly isolated. As the Pashtuns marched from Herat in June 1880, the would-be emir Muhammad Ayub Khan gathered more warriors to his banner until his forces numbered somewhere around 25,000.

Hoping to cut off what he thought was Muhammad Ayub's advance guard, Brigadier General George Burrows marched from Kandahar with 2,500 British and Indian troops to check them at the Maiwand Pass. The two sides exchanged artillery fire for three hours, and it was only when the British guns were withdrawn to replenish, and the Afghans poured in did Burrows realise the scale of the defeat he had blundered

into. The British left collapsed, leaving only the 66th (or the Berkshire) Regiment of Foot standing amid the routed sepoys. In that gloriously futile manner of which the Victorians were so proud, Colonel Galbraith ordered the Colours - the twin banners representing the regiment and the monarch - raised, and they held their ground. Galbraith was killed almost immediately, the 66th were separated into small groups ➤➤

BELOW: The 9th (Queen's Royal) Lancers, who arrived late to the Battle of Kandahar, having been sent to cut off the Afghan retreat and then recalled, put the stragglers to flight.

ABOVE: The negotiators of the Treaty of Gandamak, 1879. Second from the left is the ill-fated British Resident in Kabul, Major Sir Louis Cavagnari, and second from the right, the short-lived emir Muhammad Yaqub Kahn.

LEFT: Sher Ali Khan, son of the legendary Dost Muhammed Khan, pictured in 1869.

The conclusion of the Second Anglo Sikh War (see page 54) gave British India a not entirely welcome border with Afghanistan, the volatile North West Frontier. The restored emir of the First Anglo-Afghan War (see page 46), Dost Muhammed Khan, received his alliance with the British after all and he had remained a faithful friend even throughout the Indian Mutiny (see page 68) when many in the Afghan court had agitated for an invasion of Kashmir and Punjab.

After the events of the Crimean War (see page 60) put paid to Russian dreams of forcing open the straits to the Mediterranean, they redoubled their intrigues in Central Asia. In 1868, the Emirate of Bukhara (much of what is now Uzbekistan and Tajikistan) became a protectorate of the Russian Empire, bringing the armies of Tsar Alexander II to Afghanistan's northern border. For the new emir, Sher Ali Khan, who succeeded his father in 1863 after the requisite period of in-fighting, navigating the desires of two acrimonious great powers lurking over his northern and southern frontiers was far more acute than it had been for his predecessors. Sher Ali chose the path of absolute neutrality, but when a Russian diplomat pitched up uninvited in 1878, the viceroy of India, Robert Bulwer-Lytton, 1st Earl of Lytton demanded that Sher Ali receive a British envoy too. The emir refused.

Egged on by the British government, Lytton dispatched an invasion force, starting the Second Anglo-Afghan War (1878–1880). Sher Ali appointed his son Muhammed Yaqub Khan regent and fled the country with the Russian mission so that he might plead his case to the Tsar. Refused permission to travel onto St Petersburg, Sher Ali grew depressed, refusing food and medicine, and died in Tashkent on February 21, 1879. Muhammed Yaqub was proclaimed emir and with his father's armies scattered, he had no choice but to sign the Treaty of Gandamak (March 26, 1879). The terms allowed for a British Resident to be stationed in Kabul with authority over Afghanistan's foreign policy and transferred the vital Khyber Pass to the British, as well as two other mountain routes into British India.

Over the summer of 1879, Afghanistan chaffed under British interference and in September, the regiments of Herat returned to the capital for winter to draw their pay. His treasury emptied by the fighting, Muhammad Yaqub gave them only a third of what they were owed, and they marched on the British Residency to demand that Major Sir Louis Cavagnari make up the difference. Cavagnari stood his ground and insisted that this was a matter for the emir, not for Great Britain. The soldiers of Herat - who had heard rumours that Cavagnari was fantastically wealthy - lay siege to the Residency. Both Cavagnari and his guard fought to the last man. An expedition under Major

General Sir Frederick Roberts was quickly put together, methodically clearing the passes with troops best suited to mountain warfare. Muhammad Yaqub was effectively powerless and fled Kabul, abdicating and throwing himself at the mercy of Roberts. Showing a genuine commitment to the stability of Afghanistan, Lytton invited Abdur Rahman Khan - a first cousin of Muhammad Yaqub and grandson of Dost Muhammad - to return from exile as emir. Despite having lived as a guest of the Russian Empire, the British believed he was the best candidate to unify the country.

Sensing that it was now or never, Muhammad Ayub Khan, younger brother of Muhammad Yaqub and governor of Herat, declared himself emir, called for holy war, and marched south to Kandahar gathering tribesmen as he went.

A group portrait of Afghan warriors taken by John Burke in 1879.

RML 7-pounder Mountain Gun which could be broken down by the Royal Artillery and carried by mule. Rations were also sacrificed, with Roberts gambling that the army would be able to feed itself if they took the slightly longer route through a fertile valley.

Roberts also selected infantry he knew to be hardy, such as the 72nd (Duke of Albany's Own Highlanders) and 92nd (Gordon Highlanders) Regiment of Foot, 60th or King's Royal Rifle Corps from the British Army; and 2nd (Prince of Wales's Own), 4th, and 5th Gurkha Regiment, 2nd, 3rd, and 15th Sikh Infantry; and 23rd, 24th and 25th Punjab Infantry of the Indian Army, all recruited in mountainous regions. His cavalry brigade consisted of the 9th (Queen's Royal) Lancers, plus the 3rd Bengal Cavalry, 3rd Punjab Cavalry, and Central Indian Horse. The priority was on ammunition and fodder for the horses and mules, and even this stripped-down expedition required an awesome number of followers - perhaps as many as 9,000.

by the wave of Afghans. Further back, a single battery of Royal Horse Artillery and half a company of Bombay Sappers and Miners covered the retreat of Burrows's shattered force before they were also overrun. According to Afghan accounts - for there were no British survivors to tell the story - a small band of Berkshires, 1st Bombay Grenadiers, and Bombay Sappers and Miners, fought on from a small enclosure. When only 11 men remained alive, they charged to their deaths.

In total, over half of Burrows's force - 971 killed and 168 wounded - were amongst the casualties of the disastrous Battle of Maiwand (July 27, 1880) and the survivors limped back to Kandahar, where the garrison's commander, Lieutenant General James Primrose withdrew all British forces behind the walls and ejected the city's Pashtuns. As a seemingly trivial postscript, the loss of the Colours at Maiwand - following so soon after the disastrous Battle of Isandlwana in the Anglo-Zulu War (see page 74) - marked the last time that Colours were taken to war by British regiments.

The Long Road Round

Some 320 miles northeast in Kabul, Major General Sir Frederick Roberts resolved to move immediately. The catastrophe at Maiwand had reawoken fears of the murderous retreat from Kabul in 1842 and the thought of a similar fate befalling the defenders of Kandahar was an incentive to action. There was also the need to assure Britain's choice of emir, the newly arrived Abdur Rahman Khan (Muhammed Ayub's first cousin, both grandchildren of the popular Dost Muhammed), that they actually had the means to underwrite his rule.

From August, the citadel of Kandahar had been under almost constant bombardment and on August 16, the hapless Burrows was killed in a doomed night raid to try and silence the Afghan battery at Deh Kwaja. Roberts promised that the city would be relieved within the month and on August 8, his Kabul-Kandahar Field Force set off. They were travelling as lightly as possible. All heavy ordnance had been left in Kabul, taking only 18 light 'screw guns' such as the

ABOVE: Major General Sir Frederick Roberts circa 1880. As a result of the relief of Kandahar, he was appointed a baron and promoted to lieutenant general.

The Kabul-Kandahar Field Force was trailed almost constantly by Afghan horsemen, who hung back out of range waiting for opportunities to pick off stragglers or plunder the supplies. The dried-up riverbeds and wells provided little succour, and in any case, priority was given to the horses. Having made incredible time, Roberts allowed his weary command to rest their blistered heels for 24 hours at Gilat-il-Ghilzai, where they added the fort's small garrison to their ranks. On August 26, with 50 miles of their journey left to go, Roberts received news that Muhammed Ayub had lifted the siege and pulled back west into the hills at the threat of their arrival. On August 31, having covered 313 hard and unforgiving miles in 21 days, the jubilant relief column marched through the imposing gates of Kandahar.

Aghast at the demoralised and defeatist state of Primrose's 4,000-man garrison (Primrose would later be relieved of his post on the strength of Roberts's criticism), Roberts wasted no time in taking charge and immediately sent scouts to feel out Muhammed Ayub's new lines. ➤➤

An unknown group of British infantry pose by a road somewhere in Afghanistan. Photograph by John Burke, 1879.

The 'Last 11' die fighting at the Battle of Maiwand in this 1882 engraving.

ABOVE: The 9 (Queen's Royal) Lancers on the road to Kandahar, by Orlando Norie, 1879.

Highlanders vs Hill Tribes

The Afghan victory at Maiwand had cost Muhammed Ayub dearly, with well over 2,000 warriors slain, and if he were to fight Roberts, he was determined to do so from a position of strength. His camp was sited in the cover of a long ridged hill - bisected by Babawali Pass - which followed the line of the Argandab River. The road from Kandahar split, with the northern fork leading to the pass and the other around the end of the spur, behind which was tucked the village of Pir-E Paymal. The village, which blocked any possible advance on the Afghan camp, was invested in strength, forming a depressed centre in Muhammed Ayub's lines with his left flank on the long spur, and his right flank on a detached ridge which followed the line of the spur southwest.

At 9.30am on September 1, Roberts launched a feint against the Afghan left around the spur and the Babawali Pass using the battalions under Primrose's command, whilst the Kabul-Kandahar Field Force attacked Pir-E Paymal in a two-pronged attack, passing through the villages of Gundigan and Gundimullah Sahibabad. With the 92nd Highlanders and the 2nd Gurkhas leading the way, the villages were cleared in two hours of bitter hand-to-hand fighting and the British left pressed onto Pir-E Paymal.

By midday, the village was in British hands, with the Afghans beginning to retreat across the river. As Roberts enjoyed a celebratory glass of champagne, a final counter-attack was launched from the spur, with jezails and cannon pounding the

ABOVE: The Kabul-to-Kandahar Star, was awarded in addition to the regular Afghanistan campaign medal to those who took part in the relief march. Hsq7278 CC BY-SA 4.0

village below. Without waiting for orders - he couldn't allow his men to be shelled into a bloody pulp whilst they waited for approval - Major George White ordered bayonets fixed and the Highlanders and Gurkhas charged up the hillside and into the landslide of jezail slugs and cannon balls. Seeing many of the enemy fall, but with no sign of the attack faltering, the Afghans decided they had no desire to see what bayonets and kukris could do up close. By the time the British reached the ridgeline, the position had been abandoned completely and the battle was over.

The Iron Emir

The Battle of Kandahar brought an end to the Second Anglo-Afghan War with Muhammed Ayub Khan's camp taken, along with vast quantities of artillery and ammunition, and the deaths of 1,000 of his warriors. With only a remnant of his followers still at his side, the insurgent emir went on the run, eventually slipping across the border and into Persia.

ABOVE: A photograph of Kandahar's Durrani Gate, taken by Sir Benjamin Simpson after the fighting had ended, circa 1880-81.

The grateful Abdur Rahman accepted the terms of the Treaty of Gandamak, although the imposition of a British Resident - whose murder had sparked both Anglo-Afghan Wars to date - was quietly dropped for being too provocative to be conducive to peace. The British began their withdrawal from Afghanistan almost immediately, with Kandahar returned to the emir in 1881. As the British had predicted, Abdur Rahman had the necessary instincts to unify Afghanistan, albeit in a more cruel and tyrannical manner than the Afghans would have liked. Dubbed the 'Iron Emir', supported by a network of spies and a modern army equipped at British expense, he acted quickly to quash rebellion, displacing and exiling tribal groups who he saw as a threat, and conclusively ending any power grab by Muhammed Ayub.

Britain's judgement was tested in 1885 when conflict erupted between Russian and Afghan troops over the exact line of the border, resulting in the capture of Ak-Tepe, the fort at Panjdeh. Afghanistan's borders had always been vaguely defined and the Panjdeh Incident was part of a series of operations by which Russia deliberately

drove its frontiers further south. Under the Treaty of Gandamak, the emir was entitled to press Britain for military intervention, but wisely Abdur Rahman decided not to. He dismissed it as a border skirmish and deescalated a potential conflict between the great powers, agreeing to arbitration on the matter of the Afghan-Russian border. In 1893 he hosted the British diplomat Sir Mortimer Durand and agreed - courtesy of a significant increase in his annual subsidiary - the 1,510-mile 'Durand Line', which still marks the border between Afghanistan and Pakistan, and in 1901 the North West Frontier Province was created to represent the Pashtun majority in this corner of British India.

Within the country the legacy of Abdur Rahman is divisive, but for the British Empire his reign brought stability on the frontier and marked an urgently needed thaw in relations with the Russian Empire.

Abdur Rahman Khan, the emir of Afghanistan, pictured just prior to the war.

"Britain's judgement was tested in 1885 when conflict erupted between Russian and Afghan troops..."

BELOW: Another photograph by Simpson shows Indian soldiers camped in Kandahar's Artillery Square. The fortification in the background is the Bala Hissar (High Fort).

An 1897 etching of George William Joy's iconic painting 'Gordon's Last Stand', showing the most enduring account of his death.

Tears for Osiris

The Siege of Khartoum, March 13, 1884 – January 26, 1885

ABOVE: Egyptian khedive Isma'il Pasha whose spending bankrupted the country.

Despite a commitment to the integrity of the Ottoman Empire so strong that they were prepared to go to war for it (see page 60), France and Britain quickly became involved in the internal affairs of Egypt, an increasingly autonomous Ottoman vassal. The French began to construct the Suez Canal, whilst the British built a railway from Cairo to Alexandria, and under pressure from both, decrees banning the slave trade were passed. These were ignored and Egypt's growing prosperity depended upon unwaged labour.

Isma'il Pasha took the throne in 1863, styling himself khedive (a Persian title, meaning viceroy) and inherited a state in growing debt. Money was lavished on reforms, infrastructure projects, the lease of two Red Sea ports, the annexation of Darfur, and a catastrophic war with Abyssinia (now Ethiopia). The khedive's dream was of an empire to eclipse that of the pharaohs and he hired the charismatic Colonel Charles Gordon - feted by the British press for his adventures in Shanghai as 'Chinese Gordon' - as governor of Equatoria (part of what is now South Sudan and northern Uganda). Gordon mapped the Upper Nile and established a network of fortified trading stations, but was frustrated in his ability to quash the slave trade, thanks to the regime's indulgence of the slavers best personified by Zubayr Pasha, dubbed the 'Slaver King' and 'Black Pasha' by the British press, and the governor of Bahr el-Ghazal.

Zubayr coveted the governorship of Darfur which he had helped to conquer, and so sailed to Cairo to make his case to the khedive and demand Gordon be brought to heel. Instead, under British pressure the Black Pasha was placed under arrest and the slavers of Bahr el-Ghazal rose up, with violence spreading to neighbouring regions. Gordon, now governor-general of Sudan, broke up the slave markets, freed slaves, and saw that the ringleaders were executed, including Zubayr's son. The damage Gordon's righteous whirlwind had inflicted on Sudanese society

created a power vacuum which was filled by zealotry. In 1881 a mystic calling himself the Mahdi - the 'Expected One' promised by the Hadiths, a collection of Islamic scripture second only to the Quran - drew all of Sudan under his black flag, pledging to drive out the invader and restore Sudan to a 'purer' form of Islam. The Mahdist War (1881-1899) had begun.

Meanwhile, bankruptcy forced the khedive to sell his shares in the Suez Canal to Britain, but a year later the creditors came calling. In 1878, Britain and France took direct management of Egyptian spending with what they called 'dual control' - the installation of a British and French minister in Egypt's cabinet - and the imposition of constitutional monarchy. After attempting to exploit a military coup to resume his absolutism, Isma'il was packed off into exile and replaced by his son, Mohammed Tewfik. Another military coup by Egyptian nationalists provoked a strong reaction from the ultra-imperialist French government who perversely walked Britain's anti-imperialist Liberal government into the Anglo-Egyptian War (1882) but declined to take part themselves. The system of dual control ended with Britain exercising de facto control over a de jure province of the Ottoman Empire, all in the name of a largely ceremonial khedive.

The Mahdists now needed to be dealt with and after a force of 7,000 Egyptian soldiers under the command of Col William Hicks was slaughtered at the Battle of Shaykan (November 3-5, 1883), the British insisted on a full withdrawal from Sudan and dispatched Maj Gen Charles Gordon to Khartoum to bring the Egyptian garrison home.

ABOVE: Isma'il's son and successor, Tewfik Pasha, circa 1900.

Major General Charles Gordon was an unusual and compelling figure. Possessed of an incredible sense of moral clarity courtesy of his deep Christian faith, he was nonetheless unpredictable, highly-strung, egotistical, and prone to sudden changes in mood. His defining characteristic, however, was that he cared deeply for those in his charge.

Accompanied by a single aid, Lieutenant Colonel J. D. H. Stewart of the 11th Hussars, Gordon arrived in Khartoum on February 18, 1884, where he took charge of its 34,000 civilians and 8,000 soldiers. Nestled in the elbow of the White Nile, which ran from Lake Victoria (2,300 miles to the south), and the Blue Nile, which ran from Lake Tana (900 miles to the east), Khartoum was once the staging post for Egypt's planned conquest of Abyssinia (now Ethiopia) and the Great Lakes region (parts of what is now Burundi, Congo, Kenya, Malawi, Rwanda, Tanzania and Uganda.) Neither dream survived its collision with reality, but between 1821 and 1884, Khartoum grew into a garrison town for the Egyptian army and a crucial hub for trade.

Gordon evacuated around 2,000 women and children, sending them downriver to safety, but in his mind, his responsibility to Sudan outweighed his orders. He decided that the Mahdi must be resisted here, rather than allowed to simply rampage across the country. He dispatched countless missives

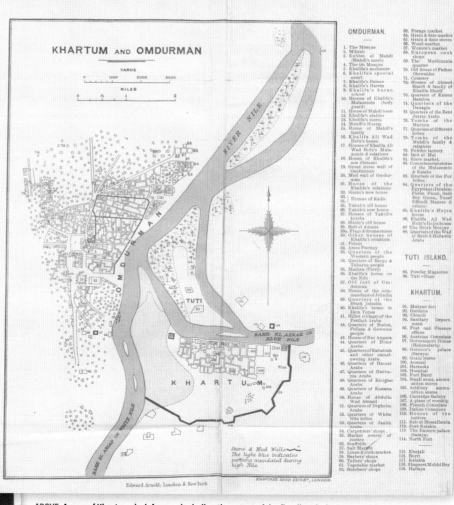

ABOVE: A map of Khartoum's defences, including the extent of the flooding during summer, from Lieutenant Rudolf Slatin's memoir, *Fire and Sword in the Sudan. A Personal Narrative of Fighting and Serving the Dervishes 1879-1895* (1896).

ABOVE: Major General Charles Gordon in the finery of an Egyptian governor-general.

to London and to the British consul in Cairo with schemes for the pacification of Sudan, the most unlikely of which was the release of Zubayr Pasha, the 'Slaver King', who he believed was the best candidate for governor. The Liberal government of prime minister William Gladstone was equivocal on the vast majority of issues, but they made a brave face of resisting the imperialist lobby. Sudan, they reasoned, was the business of Egypt and not Great Britain. They would not spend taxpayer's money on patching up the khedive's vanity project.

Pirates on the Nile

Although the Mahdi himself was somewhere far to the south, his followers were increasing, and local sheikhs followed the prevailing winds and answered the call of Jihad. It had not helped that the Egyptians were withdrawing, giving the Sudanese elites no incentive to support them. Unlike previous rebellions,

the religious character of the Mahdist revolt cut across tribal and ethnic lines. The town of Berber, some 200 miles downriver from Khartoum fell into the hands of the fanatics, blockading the Nile to boats, and on February 18, the telegraph wires were cut. Khartoum was alone and by March 13, it was surrounded by men under the command of Mohammed abu Girga, a commander appointed by the Mahdi himself.

Gordon conducted the siege with a glee suited to rip-roaring adventure fiction, which he detailed in his effervescent journals. Whilst the Mahdists were numerous, they only had a few artillery pieces and their attacks were easily waved away. Rigging up Khartoum's fleet of seven rusting paddle-steamers with wooden gun turrets and boiler-plate firing positions, Gordon's 'cavalry' - as he called them - ranged up and down the Niles collecting supplies and landing troops to raid Mahdist positions. Khartoum itself was protected by six miles of earthen ditch and parapet, four strongpoints which bristled with artillery and Maxim guns, and on two sides the Blue and White Niles presented a more formidable barrier, especially from June when the river surged

with monsoon waters from the Abyssinian highlands. The Ancient Egyptians believed this was a result of the goddess Isis weeping for her dead husband Osiris.

The Mahdi was preparing too. He appointed Khalifa Abdallahi his commander in chief and structured his zealots into divisions under different coloured flags like those of the Prophet Muhammed's armies, dressing them in white, knee-length gowns called jibbah. The Mahdist soldiers were called 'dervishes' by the British, but called themselves Ansar, meaning 'helpers', after the tribes who supported Muhammed. Curiously, Mahdi and Gordon embarked upon a correspondence, with Gordon offering him the role of governor and sending him a fez and red robe, the garb of office in the Ottoman Empire. In response, the Mahdi asked Gordon to join *him* and sent him a jibbah.

Back in Britain, the threat to Gordon was a national scandal. Finally, in August 1884 - after an intervention from Queen Victoria - General Garnet Wolseley, 1st Baron Wolseley was charged with assembling a relief force. Wolseley, who idolised Gordon, had been pushing for action for months, but he would prove no more helpful than his government. He decided to proceed up the Nile to Khartoum, as opposed to landing on the Red Sea coast and advancing overland. The chosen route was slower but safer. Time, however, is rarely on the side of the besieged.

ABOVE: A typical Mahdist warrior, or Ansari, in a white jibbah with coloured patches.

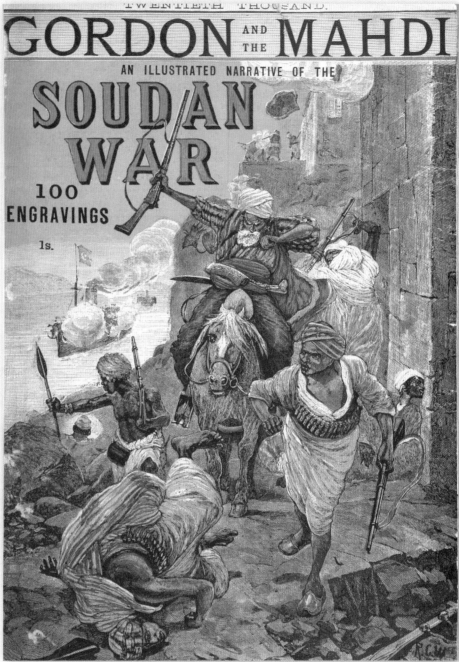

ABOVE: Gordon's steamers raid Mahdist forts on the Nile in this gung-ho cover from *Gordon and the Mahdi, an Illustrated Narrative of the War in the Soudan* (1885).

Racing the River

Whilst the swollen summer waters had enabled Gordon's pro-active defence, the threat of autumn had changed the tenor of the siege entirely. As the waters receded, they revealed mudbanks over which the Nile could be waded and increased the perimeter that Gordon's garrison needed to monitor. The 'cavalry' were also finding it increasingly difficult to secure supplies and in August one of his most competent commanders, Muhammad Ali Pasha Husayn, and 1,000 of his best soldiers were lured into an ambush and wiped out.

Concerned that the end was approaching, he arranged for Stewart to attempt a breakout aboard the steamer *Abbas* with the British and French consuls, a newspaperman, and a number of Greek refugees. Stewart was to impress upon the British the urgency of the situation. *Abbas* sailed on September 9. Two weeks later three steamers returned from a supply run along the Blue Nile with a cargo more precious than grain - news that Wolseley was on his way with 5,400 men, 3,000 travelling by river on shallow-hulled boats, and 2,400 crossing the desert as a hastily assembled Camel Corps. On October 9, he learned the Mahdi was finally on the move too with over 4,000 Ansar, but rather than be alarmed by the march on Khartoum - Gordon wrote cheerily of their looming confrontation and hoped he'd get to meet his nemesis. Two weeks later an elegant letter arrived with the Mahdi's red seal, informing Gordon in its formal but flowery Arabic ➤➤

ABOVE A cheery watercolour by Lieutenant Colonel Ernest Lomax Fraser, 3rd King's Royal Rifle Corps, of Wolseley's Nile Expedition wandering through the desert.

that *Abbas* had been captured and those who refused to convert to his cause - Stewart amongst them - killed.

The Mahdi was only a day away from Khartoum and he was persuaded to send an emissary to talk Gordon into surrendering. The 31-year-old Austrian soldier of fortune Lieutenant Rudolf Slatin had been serving as governor of Dara when he was captured. He had converted to Islam to win the trust of his men, and so his subsequent claims to have accepted the Mahdi's teachings rang true. He was, however, merely biding his time. He was the only European to have direct knowledge of the enemy's motives, plans, and the limits of his followers' loyalty,

ENGAGEMENT BETWEEN ONE OF GORDON'S ARMOURED STEAMERS AND THE REBELS POSTED ALONG THE NILE.

ABOVE The view inside one of Gordon's 'cavalry' steamers, with a wooden turret and steel plates for firing positions.

ABOVE 'Slatin Pasha', an 1896 portrait of Rudolf Slatin in the garb of a Mahdist warrior, the white jibbah with coloured squares. Wellcome Collection CC BY 4.0

and he sent a message to Gordon in German asking him to play along with the Madhi's offer. This sort of subterfuge went against Gordon's principles and to Slatin's horror, he refused his help.

Gordon's Golgotha
The exact circumstances of the fall of Khartoum and Gordon's death are unclear. His diary, the verbose primary source for the campaign, ended on December 14, but survivors spoke of supplies running out, dysentery running rampant, and Gordon running from corner to corner to supervise the defences.

Wolseley, meanwhile, had such faith in his own plan and in Gordon's ability to work miracles that he progressed with an astonishing lack of haste. Although the Camel Corps could easily have been driven on when the river column fell behind for one reason or another, they were always ordered to wait - in one case for three weeks. However, their languid rate of progress had alerted the enemy to their presence, and the Mahdi had ordered that they be slowed down and kept from Khartoum. Although the British were victorious at the Battle of Abu Klea (January 17, 1885) and the Battle of Abu Kru (January 19, 1885) against

larger numbers of Ansari, the encounters were successful in their objective of wasting Wolseley's time further.

In the pre-dawn hours of January 25, with the water low and the defenders thinned by sickness and starvation, thousands of Ansari waded through the mud of the White Nile and into Khartoum to kill and rape at will, with perhaps as many as 10,000 civilians and soldiers butchered. Despite the Mahdi's orders to take Gordon alive, he died in the battle. According to one account, after being awoken by the sounds of massacre, Gordon appeared stoically on the steps of the palace and with one hand on his sword hilt was killed by a spear through his chest. Later that day, Slatin emerged from his tent to find the sheikhs returning jubilant from the battle. One of them produced a bundle and unwrapped it, holding aloft the severed head of Maj Gen Charles Gordon, his blue eyes still half-open. It was suspended from the branches of a tree for all to admire.

An advance party from Wolseley's Nile Expedition reached Khartoum on January 28 to find black flags, rather than the red flags of Egypt awaiting them, and Mahdist cannon rather than cheering crowds. With no Gordon left to save or garrison left to evacuate, Wolseley's column withdrew. Sudan was effectively independent.

In Britain, the death of Gordon and the fall of Khartoum was a national tragedy, prompting even pointed public criticism from Queen Victoria. Stones were thrown at 10 Downing Street and

ABOVE: Lt Slatin, in chains since his failed attempted to escape and reach Gordon, is shown the severed head of the hero of Khartoum.

within two months Gladstone was forced to resign. Although he had failed to save Sudan, Gordon achieved his ambition in one respect. As the siege progressed, he increasingly viewed his role in messianic terms, referring to the coming confrontation as Armageddon - the site of the decisive battle promised in the Book of Revelations. He was described as a martyr by the British press and in the pulpit and

depicted as a saviour figure embodying the best of Christian civilisation who stood alone against a tide of Islamic 'savagery'. It was an interpretation that perfectly fit the way Britain had come to view itself and its imperial mission in the final decades of the 19th century, but one that stubbornly ignored the fact that Gordon died leading a Muslim army on behalf of a Muslim ruler to defend a Muslim people.

"One of them produced a bundle and unwrapped it, holding aloft the severed head of Maj Gen Charles Gordon."

BELOW: 'The March of the Camel Corps to Abu Klea, January 17th, 1885' in watercolour by Orlando Norie.

Imperial Reckoning

The Battle of Omdurman, September 2, 1898

In the 13 years since the Siege of Khartoum and the death of Britain's imperial martyr, Major General Charles Gordon, Egypt's army had been transformed on a grand scale. Since 1883, a senior British officer had been appointed sirdar (commander in chief) and each incumbent set about the army with the same reforming zeal as British diplomats pored over the khedive's byzantine finances.

When the time came for the energetic sirdar, Brigadier General Horatio Kitchener to move on Khalifa Abdullah, he did so at the head of a professional force of 9,000 Egyptian and Sudanese troops. The Sudanese were especially valued as whilst the Egyptians served for six year terms, the Sudanese joined for life and many were veterans of earlier conflicts. Aside from British officers and NCOs, the only European troops in

Kitchener's force were a few hundred men of the North Staffordshire Regiment and a handful of Maxim gunners.

Although this was the first army Kitchener commanded in battle - and the first campaign he had directed - he had served as second in command of the cavalry during General Garnet Wolseley, 1st Baron Wolseley's failed Nile Expedition of 1884, and he had no intention of repeating Wolseley's errors. ➤➤

BELOW: **The charge of the 21st Lancers, which accounted for over half of the British casualties in the Battle of Omdurman. A colour lithograph from the original by Stanley Berkeley, 1898.**

The Battle in Context

ABOVE: The Emin Pasha Relief Expedition crashes through the jungle interior towards Equatoria from the Congo Free State. Wellcome Collection CC BY 4.0

In the immediate aftermath of the Siege of Khartoum (see page 88), the British withdrawal from Sudan sounded like a thunderclap of divine providence. All but a handful of border forts and the remote province of Equatoria (now South Sudan), shielded by swamp, were in the hands of the Mahdists. On June 22, 1885, the Mahdi died - most likely from typhus - and Khalifa Abdullah declared himself the natural successor.

Despite periodic calls to 'avenge Gordon', the British government remained largely dispassionate about African adventures. The occupation of Egypt was not for its own sake, and after careful husbandry of the state's finances finally wiped the khedive's deficits in 1887, Britain agreed to a three-year timetable for their withdrawal.

Escalation came not by the Khalifa's hand, nor the hand of the British government, but from the other European powers. They looked on the British withdrawal from Sudan as an abdication and immediately began circling. Early in 1896, King Leopold II of Belgium, who ran the Congo Free State as his own private circle of hell, sponsored an expedition through Central Africa to Equatoria to offer the governor, Mehmed Emin Pasha, a stipend in exchange for raising the Belgian flag and keeping the line to the Congo open through the dense, cannibal-populated jungle interior. Equatoria was on the brink of falling to the Mahdists and all the expedition achieved was the deaths of over half of the team and the devastating spread of African sleeping sickness (African trypanosomiasis).

The Belgian king sponsored two further expeditions and at the Battle of Rejaf (February 17, 1897) the Free State forces defeated a larger Mahdist army to gain control of a pocket of land called the Lado Enclave, connecting the Congo to the White Nile. Perhaps the most worrying imperial machinations came from France. Still sore from their exclusion from Egypt by the British occupation, in 1896 a French military expedition left Brazzaville in the French Congo to capture Fashoda (now Kodok, South Sudan) from where they could seize the White Nile.

Last and definitely least, Italy had been drawn into the Mahdist War (1881-1899) by raids into Italian Eritrea. To the surprise of the European powers, Italian colonial troops delivered four victories over the Mahdists, drove the Ansar back into Sudan, and captured the border town of Kassala, 400 miles east of Khartoum. Flushed with confidence, the First Italo-Ethiopian War (1894-1896) was launched, ending in a crushing defeat at the Battle of Adwa

(March 1, 1896). Italian forces in Eritrea were now severely weakened and there was a possibility of a Mahdist resurgence. French arms and advisors had been crucial to the Abyssinian victory, stoking British fears of France advancing down the Blue Nile as well as the White. The prime minister, Robert Gascoyne-Cecil, 3rd Marquess of Salisbury, immediately issued instructions for the re-occupation of Sudan.

BELOW: A mounted Ansar commander depicted in wash by Richard Caton Woodville, 1896.

ABOVE: Brigadier General Horatio Kitchener, in the uniform of the commander in chief (sirdar) of the Egyptian army, confers with a British diplomat in Cairo. Wash by Richard Caton Woodville, 1896.

desert using the caravan route from Korti as Wolseley had done over a decade earlier. He began to concentrate his forces at Omdurman and further down the Nile at Abu Klea and Metemma. The sudden appearance of a British railway to his immediate north prompted the skittish Ansar commander at Berber to abandon the position entirely. Kitchener obliged him by pushing the railway into Berber by the autumn of 1897. Three battalions of British regulars were deployed for the final phase of the campaign and over the next year they shrugged off the Khalifa's raids, with the Anglo-Egyptian forces delivering a decisive defeat to the Ansari at the Battle of Atbara (April 8, 1898).

Khalifa Abdullah abandoned all ambitions of halting Kitchener's march. All the attempts so far had been met with defeat, he was losing faith in his commanders, but had not lost faith in Allah. He had heard an old prophecy that the infidel would meet his destruction at Karari just outside the city walls, and the signs so far were that Kitchener's progress was surely God's will.

Rolling Thunder

On September 1, 1898, 50,000 Ansar in their gleaming white robes gathered on the plains of Karari, banners fluttering in the warm breeze. Despite the 13 years Khalifa Abdallahi had been granted to develop and secure his Mahdist state, he had baulked at parlaying

Kitchener made his priority the construction of a railway to circumvent the vast stretches of the Nile that the seasons might render impassable, particularly the vast loop around the Nubian Desert called the Great Bend. Using soldiers and convict labour working around the clock, by October 31, 1896, the Sudan Military Railway cut across 230 miles of Nubian Desert from Wadi Halfa to Abu Hamad, reducing the travel time from 18 days to 24 hours. Whilst the British government fretted about the French expedition to Fashoda and what it might mean for control of Sudan, Kitchener was concerned only with avenging Gordon. As far as he was concerned, he could take his time, batting aside cholera, typhoid, political pressure, and Mahdist raids as if they were mosquitos.

Death on the Nile

Now able to build up troops and supplies at Wadi Halfa, 760 miles south of Cairo and 630 miles north of Khartoum, Kitchener pushed relentlessly up the Nile over the summer of 1896, capturing Dongola and receiving a promotion to major general. Although a relatively unknown officer at the start of the campaign, remarkable primarily for his command of Arabic, Kitchener's campaign was followed in detail by the British press.

The taking of Dongola suddenly left the Mahdist capital Omdurman, across the Nile from the ruined Khartoum, vulnerable and the khalifa anticipated a march south-southeast across the

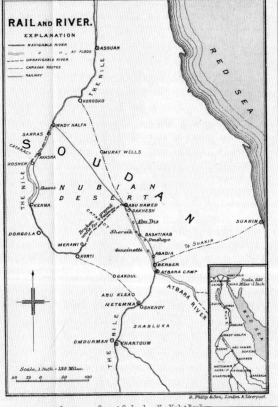

ABOVE: A map of Kitchener's Sudan Military Railway from Winston Churchill's account of the campaign, The River War (1899).

ABOVE: A 1913 illustration of an Ansar charge, with the majority of the Mahdist troops armed with spears.

with the infidel for rifles as the Abyssinian king had done, and only a fifth of his force carried firearms, mostly obsolete Remington Rolling Block rifles captured from Egyptians in the 1880s. Although numbering only 25,000 - six brigades in all - the British were armed with the new bolt-action .303 Lee-Metford rifles and the Egyptians with the quick-loading Martini-Henry that it had only just replaced.

What is more, 12 gunboats lurked on the Nile, ready to lend their cannon. The flotilla manoeuvred to within range of Omdurman and ploughed high explosive shells into its mud walls, striking with accidental but highly potent symbolism, the ivory white dome of the Mahdi's tomb. Kitchener, who had far more confidence fighting geography than he did dervishes, held back to let the khalifa dictate how the battle would be fought.

Just before dawn on September 2, the great Mahdist army began to advance as the Khalifa hastened his date with destiny. Kitchener's men lay behind a zeriba, a tangled stockade of thorns, with their backs to the Nile. Faith birthed folly as for the first few hours the Ansari charged into the jaws of the British and Egyptian artillery, the hills echoing with their rhythmic chant of the shahada: "There is no God but Allah and Muhammed is his prophet." At 2,000 yards, British Lee-Metfords joined the cannon, followed by the Maxim,

and at 600 yards the Egyptian and Sudanese troops opened fire with their Martini-Henrys. For the first time, the British fired Mark IV hollow point bullets, called 'dum-dums', which had softer tips and expanded on contact to leave horrific trauma in their wake.

With heaps of dead and clouds of smoke drifting across the plain, Kitchener ordered an advance - a reckless move with huge numbers of the khalifa's forces still unaccounted for and masked by the hills. The 21st Lancers - amongst them a young Lieutenant Winston Churchill - galloped on ahead to feel out the field, whilst the army formed into echelon (a staggered diagonal line) by brigade. Keen to get stuck in, the 400 lancers stumbled across what they thought were only a few hundred dervishes and charged what turned out to be closer to 2,500 hidden in ambush. At a cost of 70 human casualties, 119 equine casualties, and three Victoria Crosses, the gallant but guileless Lancers managed to drive off the Ansari. ➤➤

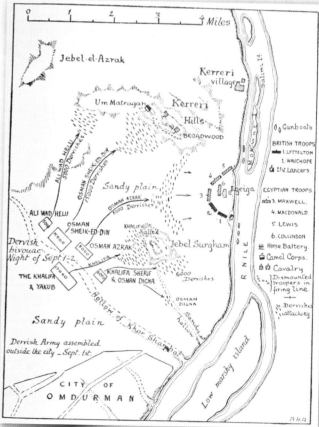

ABOVE: This map shows the Ansar assault against the zeriba in *Famous Modern Battles* (1913) by A. Hilliard Atteridge.

ABOVE: A panorama of the British-held left of the Anglo-Egyptian lines during the first attack. The men are shown wearing red coats for purposes of identification.

The Killing Blow

The British advance and the charge of the 21st Lancers - popularly but incorrectly believed to be the last cavalry charge by the British army - bought the khalifa time to bring in his reserves. As the Anglo-Egyptian echelon followed the Lancers south towards Omdurman, 17,000 men under the khalifa himself advanced from behind the advance around the Jebel Surham (the Black Hill) from the southeast and another 20,000 emerged from over the Kerreri Hills to the north.

Kitchener's two front brigades had been so focused on the prestige of being first into Omdurman that they had pulled almost a mile ahead of the rearmost brigade, which was now in the eye of the storm as Ansari converged on the Anglo-Egyptian right. The 1st Egyptian Brigade held themselves steady against this sudden reversal, credit to the hoary Brig Gen Hector MacDonald, and the echelon began to wheel to the west to cover MacDonald's left flank, Kitchener tossing them across the battlefield like toy soldiers. Fortunately for the 1st Egyptian Brigade - 2nd Egyptian Battalion, and IX, X and XI Sudanese Battalions (confusingly the Sudanese regiments were numbered

in Roman numerals and the Egyptians not) - the Mahdists were unable to co-ordinate their attacks, and MacDonald rebuffed each one in turn, before the Egyptian cavalry chased them off.

ABOVE: An Egyptian cavalryman, equipped as a British lancer with lance and carbine, depicted in wash by Woodville.

By 11.30am over 10,000 white-clad fallen littered the desert at a cost of only 48 Anglo-Egyptian dead and 382 wounded. The khalifa had escaped, but his army had been crushed, Kitchener razed the Mahdi's tomb to the ground - allegedly taking his skull to use as an inkstand until an appalled Queen Victoria intervened and had it buried - and on September 4, 1898, they sailed across to the forlorn remains of Khartoum. A memorial service for Gordon was held, the flags of Egypt and of Great Britain were hoisted, and the khedival anthem played, followed by *God Save the Queen*, and concluding with Gordon's favourite hymn, *Abide with Me*. Kitchener, according to some observers, wept.

Captain Marchand, I Presume?

His duty done, Kitchener opened a set of sealed orders from the British prime minister, Robert Gascoyne-Cecil, 3rd Marquess of Salisbury. They instructed him that once Khartoum had been retaken, he was to proceed towards Fashoda and if the French were present, ask them politely to leave. He set off with a small force of 100 Cameron Highlanders, two battalions of Sudanese infantry, and five gunboats to see if he could prevent a war, or start one.

The French were indeed present at Fashoda. On July 10, 1898 a small party of barely a

hundred tirailleurs, French colonial troops, and a handful of Europeans under the swashbuckling naval officer Captain Jean-Baptiste Marchand arrived at Fashoda, the overgrown remnant of an Egyptian fort on an island of reeds deep in the marsh. The local chief allowed them to raise the tricolore but warned them the Ansar would soon return. Soon enough, the Ansar steamed along the Nile on two of the steamers captured from Khartoum in 1884, but armed with the latest rifles, entrenched, and concealed by the reeds, the tirailleurs outranged and outmatched the larger force of over a thousand dervishes and sent them wheezing northwards to sanctuary.

The French had dug in, fearful of whatever had come next. They reinforced their trenches and heaped up earthen escarpments, and when panicked locals streaked past with news that ships had been sighted, the French took up their positions to await the wrath of the khalifa.

On the morning of September 18, two Sudanese soldiers in khaki drill uniforms and the blood red fez-like tarboosh of the Egyptian army saluted primly and handed Marchand a letter written politely in French. It extended the sirdar's greetings but informed him that he was now on his way to reclaim the khedive's rightful territory. Marchand politely disagreed. A few hours later, the two men met and outlined their incompatible stances, but both agreeing that this was a ➤➤

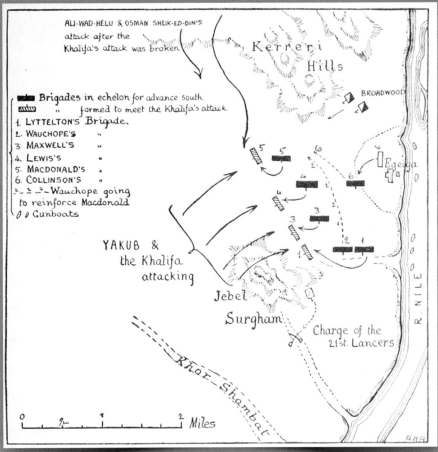

ABOVE: This map shows the second phase of the battle as the Anglo-Egyptian echelon formation comes under attack, from *Famous Modern Battles* (1913). BELOW: 'A Second Balaklava Charge' showing the 21st Lancers ploughing into a mass of Ansari. The cavalry is incorrectly depicted in their blue home service uniforms.

matter for London and Paris, and not worth shedding blood over in a swamp. Kitchener agreed that the tricolore could remain flying, whilst Marchand allowed the red khedival flag to be flown, but not the Union flag. The British brought out lukewarm whiskey and soda, and the French provided champagne, and then Kitchener sailed off to plant his flag 50 miles to the south.

After a decade of belligerent French colonial policy, they had found themselves isolated and the importance of Britain as an ally against Germany overtook the need to restore their influence over Egypt. The warlike timbre of both nations' press startled the French government, who lacked the means to force the issue of Fashoda, and they had to find a way to deescalate a situation that they themselves had brought to a boil. Marchant was withdrawn and Britain took undisputed possession of Sudan, albeit with the fiction of an Anglo-Egyptian joint venture. The French and British governments agreed on precise spheres of influence: west of the Congo was the business of France, and they were given carte blanche to carve up the rest of northwest Africa. From the brink of war to the brink of friendship in a matter of years, this understanding between the continent's paramount colonial powers allowed both empires to grow and prosper, whilst paving the way for an Anglo-French entente in 1904.

LEFT: Kitchener looks on solemnly as the British flag is raised above the ruins of Khartoum. Wash by Woodville.

BELOW: The British 1st Brigade leaves the camp behind the zeriba for the march on Omdurman. Wash by Frank Dodd, 1798.

The Black Week

The Battle of Colenso, December 15, 1899

General Sir Redvers Buller arrived in South Africa on October 31, 1899, for his first battle in 15 years to find that events had set the tempo of what should have been the crowning achievement of a long and distinguished career. A Victoria Cross hero of the Anglo-Zulu War (1879), Buller had risen in the shadow of more inspired generals and seemingly by merit

of his longevity, found himself running an entire campaign. He felt this pressure keenly, admitting in private his reservations about commanding the 1st Army Corps. His original plan had been to push north into the Orange Free State from Cape Colony, and from there ascend the gentle gradient of the high veldt - the inland plateau - of the Transvaal Republic. His

plan hadn't accounted for the Boers themselves, who laid siege to the frontier town of Mafeking and the diamond capital of Kimberley in the north of Cape Colony and cut off the garrison in Ladysmith and crossed the Tugela River into Natal. Elsewhere, Boer commandos were pushing across the Orange River and into Cape Colony, stirring up insurrection amongst ➤➤

BELOW: A highly stylised depiction of an attempt to recover the guns at the Battle of Colenso. In the actual event, the Boer fire was far more distant, but it captures the desperation and carnage.

The Battle in Context

'The Last Man of the Family' by Edward J. Austen, showing a commando heeding the call during the First Boer War.

Ever since Great Britain had acquired the Dutch station at the southern tip of Africa in the wake of the French Revolutionary Wars (1792-1802), the colonial government of Cape Colony had been on a collision course with the Boers (or Afrikaners), resilient and self-reliant settler-farmers of Dutch descent. Their austere 17th century brand of the Protestant faith recast them as a chosen people on a search for the promised land and they treated both the fertile African grasslands and its black population as a resource granted to them by God.

Great Britain's reinvention of itself as a moral superpower (however compromised) resulted in the end of slavery, improved conditions for black labourers on Boer farms, and even allowed Africans to vote and to testify against Afrikaners in court. To escape this assault on their way of life, over the 1830s great wagon trains of 'trek Boers' moved further inland to settle their own republics, two on South Africa's vast inland plateau called the high veldt, and one on the eastern coast. The latter, the short lived Natalia Republic was annexed in 1843 and Britain contented itself with economic dominance over the former, the landlocked Orange Free State and South African Republic, or Transvaal Republic which relied upon British ports in Natal and Cape Colony to export their goods.

This hands-off approach came under strain in 1866 with the discovery of a diamond field on the border of the Orange Free State. British settlers arrived in Kimberley in huge numbers and the town grew rapidly over land claimed by the Boers but occupied by Cape Colony. More disquieting for the Boers, the demands for black labour on the diamond fields drew away seasonal workers from their farms and although poorly paid, it was better than they received tending crops and cattle, and they returned able to afford their own farms and guns. After the incompetent Transvaal government bankrupted itself with a disastrous frontier war and a fruitless railway project, the British moved in and, supposedly with the consent of the citizens, annexed Transvaal in 1877. Most of the Volksraad, the Boer parliament, acquiescence in exchange for government stipends but a few hold-outs, including the stern Paul Kruger, held true to their principles and hostility to the new British administration coalesced around them. Following the Anglo-Zulu War (see page 74), the Transvaal Boers watched the British

disaster at Isandlwana with great interest, and as soon as the last of the troops had been withdrawn the First Boer War (1880-1881) was declared. After the poorly prepared British were decisively beaten by the highly mobile Boers, who raised local regiments called 'commandos' from all the available fighting-age men, the independence of Transvaal was restored.

The status quo was rocked again with the discovery of gold in Transvaal, around which the settlement of Johannesburg soon boomed. Not only was Transvaal now displacing Cape Colony as the centre of southern Africa's universe, but huge numbers of Britons and other Europeans had settled in the republic, especially around Johannesburg where they took credit for developing the town's infrastructure and the gold fields. Despite the enormous wealth now flowing into Transvaal's coffers, the 'uitlanders' (outlanders) were denied voting rights by the Volksraad who worried that it would amount to a British invasion by ballot. This was massaged into a full-blown crusade by the British high commissioner to South Africa, Sir Alfred Milner, and the secretary of state for the colonies, Joseph Chamberlain, who used the issue as pretext for war. With the support of his Orange Free State counterpart, Transvaal president Paul Kruger was willing to compromise to avert war, but this was not the outcome either Milner or Chamberlain desired. Troops en route to British India were diverted to Natal, taking up positions beyond the northmost town of Ladysmith, whilst the 1st Army Corps was formed in Britain under the command of General Sir

Redvers Buller who had fought in both the Anglo-Zulu War and the First Boer War. His patience now sorely tested, Kruger took the initiative and demanded that Britain recall its troops, and when it failed to do so the two Boer republics reluctantly declared war. Mobilising swiftly, the Boers pushed across the borders and into the exposed northwestern corner of Natal to attack the British forces at the Battles of Talana Hill (October 20, 1899) and Elandslaagte (October 21, 1899), before moving on to besiege Ladysmith. In the southwest, they crossed the borders into Cape Colony to lay siege to Mafeking - the rail hub to the north - and Kimberley.

LEFT: Stephanus Johannes Paulus 'Paul' Kruger, four-times elected President of the South African Republic (Transvaal), photographed in 1900.

ABOVE: Sir Redvers Buller in the uniform of a colonel, 1882.
Courtesy of the Royal Collections Trust

the Cape Afrikaners. He had set out for South Africa with the intention of invading two nations but was now facing an invasion of two of his own.

That Buller had his doubts about the deployment of the British forces in Natal - they were, in his opinion too far forward and too easily encircled - and that he had been proven correct was no comfort at the cost of 12,500 soldiers bottled up uselessly in Ladysmith. Perhaps more worrying in hindsight was not that he had worried about this very possibility, but he had done nothing to correct the situation and had left Lieutenant General Sir George White to his own devices. Buller was an excellent motivator of soldiers and a superb tactician, but he was an indecisive strategist and too eagerly offloaded his awesome responsibilities onto those who desired them.

Buller's original strategy now had to be changed. Ladysmith needed to be urgently relieved. A division of 8,000 men under Lt Gen Paul Stanford, Lord Methuen was to make haste for Kimberley to relieve the diamond capital and stop Cecil Rhodes from making a nuisance of himself. A token force of 3,000 under Lt Gen Sir William Gatacre - dubbed 'back-acher'

for the way in which he relentlessly drove his men - was to resist further incursion into Cape Colony and deter Afrikaner insurrection. Buller, meanwhile, sailed to the relief of Natal and into the jewel in the imperial crown of Victorian Britain's infamous 'Black Week'.

Operational Manoeuvres in the Dark

Gatacre and Methuen were dealt crushing blows just a day apart. At the Battle of Stormberg (December 10, 1899), Gatacre tried to capture a vital railway junction 50 miles from the Orange River, beginning with a night march over unfamiliar terrain with imperfect guides who took them on a wider arc than intended. Arriving late and at the wrong place, 135 were killed and wounded, and another 600 captured in a fruitless assault on a steep hillside.

At the Battle of Magersfontein (December 11, 1899), Methuen advanced by night on expertly prepared Boer positions. Predictably they stumbled in the dark and when dawn broke, they were caught in the open. The enemy had dug in at the base of the hills with trenches that gave them a level line of fire across the

"Buller was an excellent motivator of soldiers and a superb tactician, but he was an indecisive strategist..."

BELOW: An inaccurate depiction of the 3rd (Highland) Brigade at the Battle of Magersfontein, realistic only in its depiction of the utter chaos.

Paul Sanford Methuen, Lord Methuen pictured in 1910 by which time he had been promoted to full general and appointed governor of the Colony of Natal.

Lieutenant General Sir William Forbes Gatacre, KCB, DSO pictured just before 1899.

battlefield, whilst the British were entirely ignorant of their positions until they began to take casualties. The day ended with 120 British dead and another 690 wounded.

Meanwhile in Natal, the road and railway to Ladysmith crossed the Tugela River at Colenso, which nestled in a crook of the winding river, before climbing through a steep nek linking Red Hill and Grobelaar Hill. It was being held by 5,000 Boers under the command of Gen Louis Botha. Botha covered the hillsides in trenches, many of which were left empty to deceive the British of their precise strength and disposition.

Buller had the numbers to worry the entire Boer line and he planned a noisy diversionary attack on Colenso whilst he crossed 25 miles upriver and turned the Boer flank. On December 12, he ordered up the guns to begin bombardment of the hills around Colenso and then telegraphed White in Ladysmith that he would be striking on December 17. It was a solid enough plan, but news of Stormberg and Magersfontein sent him reeling. Two costly defeats - alongside the failure to relieve Kimberley - following so sharply on one another's heels destroyed Buller's confidence in his manoeuvre entirely. Without updating Ladysmith of his thinking (or lack of), Buller fixed a new attack for December 15 and ordered his three brigades to effect a crossing at three points.

In all three cases, their orders were imprecise and based on a threadbare understanding of the terrain. On the left of the British line, Maj Gen Arthur Fitzroy Hart was to cross a drift to the west of a spruit (a small tributary) with the 5th (Irish) Brigade and push north, but there were two tributaries with drifts to their west and only one was passable on foot. In the centre, Maj Gen Henry Hildyard's 2nd Brigade was to cross the iron bridge in Colenso, but the village had two iron bridges - road and rail - which crossed at different points and only the road bridge was intact. On the right, Col Douglas Cochrane, 12th Earl of Dundonald, commanding the 1,000-man Mounted Brigade, was instructed to take the only piece of high ground on this side of the Tugela, Hlangwane Hill. Over 3,000 feet high, it was the crack in Botha's fastness, and he had been forced to leave it in the hands of a token force of defenders. Buller though, regarded it only ever as a diversion.

In reserve, covering the 5th (Irish) and 2nd Brigades was Maj Gen Neville Lyttleton's 4 Brigade, whilst Maj Gen Geoffrey Barton's 6th (Fusiliers) Brigade was instructed to cover Hildyard's right and support Dundonald if necessary.

The Darkest Day

Unlike the first two battles of 'Black Week', the Battle of Colenso began by daylight with Buller's force advancing on their targets at the first light of what would become a suffocating hot summer's day. First into battle was Col Charles Long who rushed ahead with 14th and 66th Batteries, Royal Field Artillery, and a detachment of naval guns. He was supposed to be moving in support of Hildyard's brigade, but his carriages clattered past the startled infantry to within 700 yards of the riverbank and around a mile ahead of the 2nd Brigade. Long parked his guns smartly as if readying them for inspection while the entire Boer line opened up on these tempting targets. Unbelievably, Long's guns kept firing until they had expended all of their ammunition, then with 12 of his crews killed and 29 wounded - including Long himself who took a piece of shrapnel in his liver - they withdrew. ➤➤

ABOVE: A view down the concealed Boer trench line in front of the Magersfontein hills. Zuid-Afrika Huis

Long was not the only officer to comport himself with a level of pig-headedness that went beyond parody. Maj Gen Hart, known as 'General No Bobs' as he never flinched or ducked when under fire, began to follow a well-trodden road to where one would reasonably expect to find a drift. Then, Hart took the advice of his guides that the drift was elsewhere and veered off the road to the right where the 5th (Irish) Brigade found themselves trapped in a bend of the river with Boer trenches on three sides. As murderous fire tore into the Irish, one officer tried to detach his men and search for the drift further upstream, but Hart pulled him back and urged them onward. A bugle sounded the charge and some men fixed bayonets and poured into the Tugela where they drowned. Eventually, Buller sent Lyttleton up to cover the Irish retreat and the bloodied brigade limped back for shelter having taken 532 casualties.

ABOVE: Boer artillery overlooking the Tugela River at Colenso. Zuid-Afrika Huis

ABOVE: Douglas Cochrane, 12th Earl of Dundonald, in the uniform of a junior officer in the Life Guards, circa 1870.

The dashing Lord Dundonald meanwhile had done as instructed and managed to get his dismounted Mountain Brigade to the base of Hlangwane Hill where the defenders were holding them off. His request for reinforcements from Barton was refused as Buller had by now decided to give up on his left and right flanks and concentrate entirely on the centre column at Colenso. He had by now had lost all view of the wider battle and was down at the front where he was fixated on getting Long's artillery out of a sunken, dried up riverbed where they sheltered from the Boer bombardment.

Captain Harry Schofield, Royal Horse Artillery, asked for volunteers and two staff officers stepped forward to join the limber teams of the 66th Battery.

Lieutenant the Honourable Freddy Roberts - the only son of Field Marshal Frederick Roberts, 1st Baron Roberts - was shot from his saddle after 30 yards, and Cap Walter Congreve had his horse shot out from under him, but miraculously survived and crawled to the mortally wounded Roberts. Two guns were successfully recovered, and another attempt was made at an equally heavy cost.

Seven Victoria Crosses were earned in sheer folly to reclaim the guns and confronted only with a panorama of the dead and wounded Buller judged that all was lost. Arguably it was not, other guns were available to reinforce the attack and two brigades had seen little fighting at all. Lord Dundonald could also have occupied Hlangwane with some aid from other quarters, but Buller had lost all perspective in every possible sense.

Black Week, White Future

The shock of Black Week reverberated across the empire like the clanging of funeral bells. Moves were made to remove Buller from his post, but as an immensely popular commander with the rank and file, this could only be done by degrees. Not yet aware that his only son and heir had been slaughtered, Field Marshal Frederick Roberts, 1st Baron Roberts was appointed commander in chief, whilst Buller remained in control of the Natal Field Force only. As with his dynamic march to relieve Kandahar in the Second Anglo-Afghan War (see page 82), Roberts went on to launch an audacious flanking march which took the Boers by surprise and hammered through their capitals. The demoralised Buller continued to dither his way through Natal, and it was February 28, 1900, before Ladysmith was

ABOVE: Boer pickets on the slopes of the hills around the Tugela. Zuid-Afrika Huis

LEFT: 'The Last Shot at Colenso', a fanciful scene which appears to combine Colonel Charles Long's battery firing its last shot, with the desperate attempt to withdraw the guns later in the battle.

BELOW: A map of the Battle of Colenso showing troop movements, from *The Times History of the War in South Africa* (1900).

BOTTOM: A copy of Sidney Paget's 1906 watercolour of the guns being limbered under intense fire from the Boer positions across the Tugela.

Eventually, the Boers came to terms and in the Treaty of Vereeniging (May 31, 1902) they reluctantly agreed to the annexation of Transvaal and Orange Free State with the promise of self-government at the earliest opportunity. They also received assurances that black voting rights would remain off the table for the foreseeable future. South Africa's black population - its original and still most numerous inhabitants - were abandoned by Great Britain, whose high-minded aspirations always came a very distant second to the security and prosperity of its empire.

Despite the ambition of Sir Alfred Milner who had hoped to flood the new Transvaal and Orange River Colonies with British settlers and reshape the veldt in their image, Afrikaners remained dominant. When the Union of South Africa was formed in 1910, they dominated its government too, eventually spawning the poisonous ideology of apartheid which divided South Africa for the majority of the 20th century.

relieved, by which time Roberts was well on his way to conquering Orange Free State.

For the most part, the British hadn't expected such dogged resistance from glorified mountain men and the response to the sudden reversals was a level of patriotic engagement that prefigured the mass mobilisation of World War One, with society gentlemen volunteering for Imperial Yeomanry cavalry contingents and society ladies lending their services as nursing volunteers. The reserves and the militia, which had recently been amalgamated into the 3rd and 4th battalions of the regular infantry, were also mobilised for service. Canada, New Zealand and the separate colonies of Australia (which federated during the conflict) also sent contingents of fighting men, an important step in crafting for them a new relationship within the empire, one that would be called upon increasingly heavily in the early 20th century, and a unique military heritage of their own.

With Roberts in the field, battles began to turn in favour of the British and the Boers trusted their fate to irregular warfare, which provoked steadier more cruel and repressive reprisals such as land clearances, military tribunals, and the establishment of concentration camps. And although the aim of the British concentration camps was not to cause suffering, they did so nonetheless.

A Coalition of Chaos

The Battle of Peking, August 14-15, 1900

The Legation Quarter of Beijing was wedged between the walls of the Tartar City on one side and the Outer City on the other. It was approximately two miles by a mile in size and home to 11 foreign legations, a number of foreign businesses, banks, and missionary societies. Despite the strong defensive walls which bookended the north and south, the footprint was simply too big to be defended by the 409 assorted troops and 150 armed volunteers available. The perimeter was drawn closer, with the Italian legation abandoned and its inhabitants joining the Japanese, the Austrians moving in with the French, and their vacated buildings soon set ablaze by the enemy. Being a soldier as well as a diplomat (which says much about British attitudes to China) Colonel Sir Claude Maxwell MacDonald appointed himself ➤➤

BELOW: **A French oil print showing the savage hand-to-hand fighting in defence of the British Legation in Beijing.**

ABOVE: British infantry attack their Chinese counterparts during the First Opium War (1839-1842), which ended with Hong Kong ceded to Great Britain. Watercolour by Richard Simkin.

By the close of the 19th century, China was on the brink of cultural and political collapse with the Boxer Rebellion (1900) only the most recent chapter in a long and unedifying saga. A series of natural disasters, incredible poverty, political repression, and the 'Unequal Treaties' struck by the likes of Great Britain, Russia and Japan at gunpoint had resulted in crippling reparations and the lease of great chunks of valuable territory (such as Hong Kong to Britain and Manchuria to Russia) under the most humiliating terms. In the wake of the European bankers and merchants swarmed missionaries, whose freedom of movement was assured by the Treaty of Tientsin (1861), leading to fears about the erosion of traditional Confucian values. As the only visible symbol of the forces which had forced China onto its knees in many rural parts of this vast nation, Chinese converts to Christianity were increasingly targeted by the patriotic Yihequan movement.

Meaning 'Righteous and Harmonious Fists', the Yihequan disciplined themselves with martial arts and calisthenic exercises that they believed rendered them invulnerable to bullets. Nicknamed 'Boxers' by the Westerners, they murdered Christians, tore up railway and telegraph lines, and harassed foreign diplomats and businesses.

After initially cracking down on Boxer activity and executing its leaders, the Qing government, no stranger to rebellions, maintained an attitude of studied ambiguity lest they were seen as colluding with the foreigners. Empress Dowager Cixi exercised power on behalf of her son, but possessing a formidable strength of character, she continued her regency after the Tongzhi Emperor's death aged 18. When her nephew and her son's successor, the Guangxu Emperor got a taste for wide-ranging reform

ABOVE: Empress Dowager Cixi effectively ruled China on behalf of her son and then her nephew for nearly half a century.

of everything from education to the army to the introduction of constitutional monarchy, Cixi launched a conservative coup and placed him under house arrest. Rather than being the power behind the throne, from 1861 when her husband the Xianfeng Emperor died, Cixi effectively was the throne.

The rising tensions led the British government to dispatch the Seymour Expedition (June 10-28, 1900) to protect the international residents of the Chinese capital, Peking (now Beijing). Led by the Royal Navy's Vice Admiral Edward Seymour and consisting of 2,000 mostly naval personnel from an alliance of colonial powers, just under half of which were British Royal Marine Light Infantry. Landing in Tianjin, they commandeered five trains and set off for Beijing. However, not having bothered to ask the Qing government, it effectively constituted an invasion. The Chinese Army, the Kansu Braves - a Muslim Chinese unit loyal to the Qing dynasty and used as Beijing's civil defence force - and the Boxers beat them back. Seymour withdrew lighter by 62 dead and heavier by 232 wounded.

Empress Dowager Cixi ordered that the foreign legations leave and organised a Chinese military escort to take them to Tianjin, however in the tense, fast-moving events a German diplomat was killed by one of the guards, and the rest of the internationals frantically barricaded themselves into their compounds. On June 21, deciding that she now had nothing to lose but everything to gain, Cixi sided with the Boxers and declared war on all foreign powers. Chinese Christians and foreigners alike rushed to Beijing for their own protection and sealed off the Legation Quarter of the city.

ABOVE: A stereoscopic photograph of guards outside the Russian Legation, 1901.

commander of the Legation Quarter's defence, although each continent of foreign troops acted semi-independently. Three miles away at the ornate Beitang Roman Catholic Cathedral, a small party of French and Italian soldiers, priests, nuns, and more than 3,000 Chinese Christians endured their own siege no less valiantly, but with much less publicity.

The efforts of the besieging army - consisting of the Boxers, the Kansu Braves, and the Chinese regulars - were uncoordinated, and the commander of the Peking Field Army strongly disapproved of his government's policy leading to a steady stream of collapsing ceasefire proposals that at least helped ease the pressure on the Legation Quarter's defenders. The terrain of

the Chinese capital, grand houses, parks, and tightly packed streets, all contributed to the intensity of the fighting and each 'front' faced a unique challenge.

At one point, the 15th-century Hanlin Academy, home to many rare volumes, was set ablaze to try and burn the British Legation out and the British braved sniper fire to try and extinguish the neighbouring inferno.

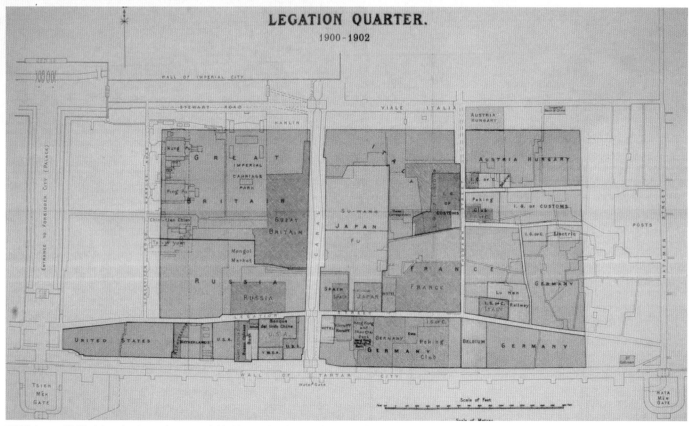

ABOVE: A map of Beijing's Legation Quarter in 1900 overlaid with 1902 when the zones became exclusive to the international community.

ABOVE: A French lithograph showing the defenders of the Legation Quarter with one of their three machine guns, 1900.

The Su Wang Fu (known simply as 'The Fu'), a mansion and park in the northeast corner which its owner Prince Su had turned over to the refugee Chinese Christians, was defended by the Japanese commander Lieutenant Colonel Shiba Gorō, whilst the French Legation at the easternmost point was only 50 feet from the enemy trenches and subject to tunnelling. The 50-foot tall Tartar Wall to the south, which separated the Legation Quarter from the Outer City, was held by US Marines and German troops, and they fought bitterly to keep it from falling into Chinese hands from where they would be able fire indiscriminately into the buildings below. Walls are only defensible if you hold them all and despite building barricades, the American and German defenders were vulnerable to sniper fire from the towers along the walls and from the rooftops of nearby houses. On June 30, a Chinese assault on the ramparts took the Germans by surprise and they withdrew in panic, leaving their positions to be occupied by the Chinese. With the US Marines now dangerously exposed and the Chinese creeping steadily closer, a few days later an all-or-nothing American-led counter-attack of US, Russian and British troops charged over their barricades in the cover of darkness. Catching the Chinese sleeping, they killed dozens and retook the crucial stretch of wall.

By July 13, the Japanese lines at the Su Wang Fu had been pushed back and a mine was detonated beneath the French Legation, driving the defenders almost entirely out of the ruins. A third of the available fighting men had been made casualties.

"Not Massacred Yet"

Whilst a handful of diplomats and a few hundred soldiers held one of Asia's largest land empires at bay the Eight-Nations Alliance - Great Britain, Russia, Germany, France, Austria-Hungary, Japan, Italy and the United States - quickly put together a relief force of 8,000 Japanese, 4,800 Russians, 3,000 British (mostly British Indian Army), 2,100 Americans, and 500 French troops. The Austrian, Italian and German contributions were negligible. Relieving the Legation Quarter was no simple task, as the Seymour Expedition had discovered. To reach the defenders they would have to make their way through two walls via well-guarded gatehouses and brave the streets, home to a population whipped into a frenzy by the xenophobia of the Boxers.

On July 28 a young boy slipped through the cordon and delivered a message that the Eight-Nation Army was marching from Tianjin. Asked to carry back an update on the defenders, a British soldier suggested laconically: "Not massacred yet." Truth was that whilst the Legation Quarter had stubbornly resisted the bullets and barrages of the Chinese, they were rapidly running out of food. Whilst the Europeans and Japanese held their noses and served up horse flesh, the 2,812 Chinese Christians who had sought sanctuary were forced to chew bark and fend off smallpox on empty stomachs.

The limits of coalition warfare between such a disparate group were quickly making themselves felt. The Russians refused to serve under a British or French officer on point of pride; the French argued that the British had already used up their turn on the Seymour Expedition; and although Japan provided the largest contingent and had the most senior commander by rank, none of the Europeans could contemplate the leadership of a non-European. As a diplomatic fudge, Germany's Field Marshal Alfred von Waldersee ➡➡

ABOVE: 'Some of China's troublemakers' - a photograph of captured Boxers.

sweltering heat, the Chinese were defeated again at Battle of Yangcun (August 6, 1900) and the road to Beijing was left open. This was not the same determined defiance that the Seymour Expedition had faced where horrified soldiers reported that it often took as many as three shots to bring down a fanatical Boxer. As with the siege of the Legation Quarter, the Chinese army was little convinced of the benefits of this conflict. This was fortunate for the allies, as both battles had exposed a woeful absence of co-operation between the foreign powers. At Beicang, the Japanese saw an opportunity and pushed on, seizing the initiative and routing the Chinese almost entirely by themselves, whilst at Yangcun the Russians shelled their own allies under British direction as a consequence of the latter measuring distance in yards and the former in metres. It had all the recipes of a massacre had they been facing anything other than the anachronistic and profoundly demoralised army of China.

The Rush for the Gates

On August 14, the hot, weary, and significantly thinned Eight-Nation Army was scheduled to make its first demonstrations against the eastern walls of Beijing. The plan was for the Russians to take the northernmost gate of the Tartar City, then the Japanese, and then the French; on the other side of the Imperial Canal, the gates of the Outer City would be assailed by the Americans, and then the British. Now, in addition to the expected

was appointed on the basis that with so few Germans in the field he was not in a position to favour his own forces. However, Waldersee did not actually arrive in the field until well after the Legation Quarter had been relieved, and so Britain's Major General Sir Alfred Gaselee was appointed acting commander by merit of seniority.

Gaselee argued for the immediate advance on Beijing and the Americans agreed, but the French and Russian contingents objected, worrying about the effects of the intense heat. They proposed waiting until Autumn had cooled things off (and by which time the French would have a larger contingent of troops in place, increasing their influence over the campaign) and Waldersee had taken charge. Gaselee called their bluff and said that unless they agreed, the British and Americans would advance alone. The Siege of the Legation Quarter clearly demanded urgency.

As they advanced from Tianjin, they pushed back a Chinese force at the Battle of Beicang (August 5, 1900) before driving on to the Hai River where a strong defensive line had been prepared. Fighting in the

ABOVE: A stretch of the barricaded Tartar Wall, looking down towards the bullet-riddled American Legation building.

ABOVE: A stunning 1900 Japanese wood engraving of their assault on the gates of Beijing.

"An orgy of violence followed, further deepening the divisions between the Eight-Nation Army."

chaos, the five armies were being driven to plant their proverbial flag in the Legation Quarter first as a matter of national pride. The Russian detachment had learned that the gate assigned to the Americans was lightly defended, and so on the night of August 13, they crossed the Imperial Canal and attacked the American target in force, seizing the gatehouse and blasting a hole into the gate itself.

Having not bothered to inform their allies of the decision, the effect was twofold. Firstly, without any support, the Russians were pinned down by the Outer City's defenders and suffered so heavily they were unable to advance any further. Secondly, the sound of the attack prompted a dash by the other armies. Upon discovering the Russians were blocking their route, the Americans scaled the walls instead. The British found that their gate was lightly guarded courtesy of the Russians drawing all the defenders into the northeast corner. They blasted it open and moved into the Outer City to little resistance. There they discovered a drainage ditch which led directly into the Legation Quarter. Wading through the slurry, the British - Rajputs and Sikhs of the British Indian Army - were the first to reach the defenders. The Japanese, despite their pluck and professionalism, were armed only with light artillery and battering the gate open took longer than expected. Once inside they found that

without the Russians to their north, they were facing almost all of the Tartar City's defenders.

Boxing Clever

An orgy of violence followed, further deepening the divisions between the Eight-Nation Army. All of the armies took part in looting to one degree or another, although the Americans tried to stifle it in their own men. The British had a system for loot, which was only taken from empty properties or known enemies and auctioned with the profits, or 'prize', distributed in accordance with rank.

The Russians and Germans gained particular notoriety for their brutality towards civilians. Waldersee, once he had arrived and taken charge, found plenty of work for the German reinforcements, sweeping the city block by block in search of suspected Boxers. Although many people were killed, evidence that any of them were rebels remained conspicuous for its absence. With a miserable inevitability, an uprising born out of the inequality of foreign treaties ended with one. The Boxer Protocol entitled all of the participating powers to station their armies in China, and extorted reparations for property damage and the like which exceeded the entire state budget. In Beijing, the Chinese were forbidden from living in the Legation Quarter, from gathering in groups larger than three, and subject to

strict curfews. Anti-foreign societies were criminalised, and the import of weapons was banned for two years.

Although Cixi was compelled to stand down for her role in the Boxer Rebellion, the Qing Dynasty limped on for another decade before finally collapsing in 1912. China became a republic, before crumbling into a long and bloody civil war in 1927, one that barely paused with World War Two, before resuming in earnest until 1950.

Although the Battle of Peking was a victory for the imperial powers, it was one which brought much of the ugliness of imperialism into the light. The carnage of summary executions forced many in the west to weigh up just who the 'savages' were. The behaviour of the Germans had been underscored by a rousing speech from the unstable and incendiary Kaiser Wilhelm II which horrified even the German government who released an edited version with the more bloodthirsty rhetoric omitted: "Should you encounter the enemy, he will be defeated! No quarter will be given! Prisoners will not be taken! Whoever falls into your hands is forfeited. Just as a thousand years ago the Huns under their King Attila made a name for themselves, one that even today makes them seem mighty in history and legend, may the name German be affirmed by you in such a way in China that no Chinese will ever again dare to look cross-eyed at a German."

The Twilight of Empire

From the World Wars to Independence

Over 150 years of Britain's battles for an empire eventually took the nation to 1914 and 1939, where it would fall to the empire to battle for Britain. Thanks to the comprehensive reforms which followed the Indian Mutiny, the British Indian Army of 1914 was one of the most professional fighting forces in the world and in 1915 it arrived in Europe for the first time to reinforce the battered British Expeditionary Force on the Western Front. The empire grew to its greatest territorial extent in the wake of World War One, flushed with protectorates plucked from the ribcage of the defeated Ottoman and German Empires, but the experiences of this war also marked the beginning of the end. Independence movements were energised by the eruption of the Bolshevik Revolution, the subjugated peoples of eastern and southeastern Europe realised their dreams of statehood, and the limitations of Great Britain to protect itself and its empire had become all too clear.

The British Indian Army - the largest volunteer army that the world had ever seen - served again in 1939 - along with fighting men from Africa, the Caribbean, Australia, New Zealand, and Canada. The empire fed Britain through the darkest days of the World War Two, built its warships, crewed its merchant fleet, marched in its columns, and serviced its Spitfires, but after 1945 the debt was marked as paid in full. Indian officers who watched British soldiers break and flee at Singapore had little awe left for the great King-Emperor over the sea, whilst black airmen from the West Indies discovered a sad, drab little country far removed from the glittering global capital they had imagined from childhood. A wave of decolonisation followed the peace, and, in many cases, the empire's step-children retained little love for their step-father and all too eagerly severed ties, whilst others boarded ships and returned 'home'.

ABOVE: Men of the Gold Coast Regiment (from what is now Ghana), part of the Royal West African Frontier Force, take a break on the road in 1942. Men of the Gold Coast Regiment fought in Italian Somaliland and then against the Japanese in Burma.

Whether World Wars were the empire's finest moments or its darkest is still fiercely disputed and well outside of our scope, but they were undeniably its final moments. A true product of empire, Mahatma Gandhi received his political awakening as a lawyer in South Africa, where many Indians laboured as indentured servants to the Boers. He played a vital role in forming a volunteer ambulance corps with which to assist the British Army during the Second Boer War and prove the worth of his community. He wrote of his motivations in 1924: "If we desire to win our freedom and achieve our welfare as members of the British Empire, here is a golden opportunity for us to do so by helping the British in the war by all means at our disposal."

He was speaking of the Indian inhabitants of South Africa, but by the 1940s those words could have been uttered by any one of the 2.5 million Indian soldiers, seamen and airmen who served, as well as their counterparts from Africa, the Caribbean, and beyond.